SQL Server on Linux

Configuring and administering Microsoft's database solution

Jasmin Azemović

BIRMINGHAM - MUMBAI

SQL Server on Linux

Copyright © 2017 Packt Publishing

First published: August 2017

Production reference: 2110817

Published by Packt Publishing Ltd.
Livery Place
35 Livery Street
Birmingham
B3 2PB, UK.
ISBN 978-1-78829-180-4

www.packtpub.com

Credits

Author
Jasmin Azemović

Reviewer
Marek Chmel

Commissioning Editor
Amey Varangaonkar

Acquisition Editor
Tushar Gupta

Content Development Editor
Cheryl Dsa

Technical Editor
Prasad Ramesh

Copy Editor
Safis Editing

Project Coordinator
Nidhi Joshi

Proofreader
Safis Editing

Indexer
Pratik Shirodkar

Graphics
Tania Dutta

Production Coordinator
Melwyn Dsa

About the Author

Jasmin Azemović is a university professor active in the database systems, information security, data privacy, forensic analysis, and fraud detection fields. His PhD degree was in modeling design and developing an environment for the preservation of privacy inside database systems. He is the author of many scientific research papers and two books: Writing T-SQL Queries for Beginners Using Microsoft SQL Server 2012 and Securing SQL Server 2012. He has been a Microsoft MVP (Data Platform) for the last 10 years and an information security consultant. He is an active speaker at many IT professional and community conferences.

I thank God for giving me the strength to write this book and not give up in hard moments. Special gratitude goes to my wife Nermana and children Selver, Imran, and Sara. They supported me even when I was spending family time working on this project. Finally, thanks go to my parents father Atif and mother Adila for encouraging me to choose an as my profession many years ago and selflessly supporting me on that path.
Finally, I'm grateful to all the people who helped me on the way and made this book possible: Travis Wright from Microsoft for pointing me in the right direction and the Packt team for recognizing the potential of this book and working with me on it: Tushar Gupta, Amey Varangaonkar, Cheryl D'sa, and Prasad Ramesh.

About the Reviewer

Marek Chmel is an IT consultant and trainer with more than 10 years' experience. He is a frequent speaker, with a focus on Microsoft SQL Server, Azure, and security topics. Marek writes for Microsoft's TechnetCZSK blog and since 2012 he has been an MVP (Data Platform). He has also been recognized as a Microsoft Certified Trainer: Regional Lead for the Czech Republic for a few years in a row. He holds many MCSE certifications, he's also an EC Council Certified Ethical Hacker and holder of several eLearnSecurity certifications. Marek earned his MSc in business and informatics from Nottingham Trent University. He started his career as a trainer for Microsoft server courses. Later, he joined AT&T as a senior database administrator, with a specialization in MSSQL Server, data platforms, and machine learning.

www.PacktPub.com

For support files and downloads related to your book, please visit www.PacktPub.com.

Did you know that Packt offers eBook versions of every book published, with PDF and ePub files available? You can upgrade to the eBook version at www.PacktPub.com and as a print book customer, you are entitled to a discount on the eBook copy. Get in touch with us at service@packtpub.com for more details.

At www.PacktPub.com, you can also read a collection of free technical articles, sign up for a range of free newsletters and receive exclusive discounts and offers on Packt books and eBooks.

https://www.packtpub.com/mapt

Get the most in-demand software skills with Mapt. Mapt gives you full access to all Packt books and video courses, as well as industry-leading tools to help you plan your personal development and advance your career.

Why subscribe?

- Fully searchable across every book published by Packt
- Copy and paste, print, and bookmark content
- On demand and accessible via a web browser

Customer Feedback

Thanks for purchasing this Packt book. At Packt, quality is at the heart of our editorial process. To help us improve, please leave us an honest review on this book's Amazon page at `https://www.amazon.com/dp/1788291808`.

If you'd like to join our team of regular reviewers, you can e-mail us at `customerreviews@packtpub.com`. We award our regular reviewers with free eBooks and videos in exchange for their valuable feedback. Help us be relentless in improving our products!

Table of Contents

Preface

Microsoft now loves Linux and part of its new exciting strategy is the availability of SQL Server as one of the best database platforms on all major Linux distributions. This book will be your quick-start guide to this new uncharted space. You will recognize and understand the full potential of a new database environment in the Linux world. At this point, the technology is pretty fresh and getting to know things now in this early phase will be to your strategic advantage.

What this book covers

Chapter 1, *Linux Distributions*, covers the basics of supported Linux distributions. You will learn about openSUSE and Ubuntu distributions and will be prepared for the installation procedure.

Chapter 2, *Installation and Configuration*, covers key points about the installation and initial configuration of SQL Server on Linux. You will learn how to install SQL Server on Linux on the openSUSE and Ubuntu distributions.

Chapter 3, *SQL Server Basics*, is about the SQL Server architecture and concepts, and how they differ from other database platforms.

Chapter 4, *Database in the Sandbox*, is about using DDL and DML sets of SQL statements in the SQL Server environment. You will learn how to create, modify, and delete a database and its objects, and how to implement INSERT, SELECT, DELETE, and update statements.

Chapter 5, *Sample Databases*, teaches you how to find and install SQL Server samples. You will learn how to restore a sample database and browse through its structure and objects.

Chapter 6, *A Crash Course in Querying*, shows you how to write efficient queries on SQL Server samples. The readers will learn to write SELECT statements on one or more tables in combination with different sets of operators and functions.

Chapter 7, *Backup and Recovery Operations*, is about understanding and creating backup procedures inside your database environment. The process of restoring is equally as important as backing up. This chapter will also teach you how to create and implement an efficient restore procedure.

Chapter 8, *User Management*, focusses on the user management process using the security features of SQL Server. You will learn how to implement new logins and map procedures to specific assets on SQL Server.

Chapter 9, *Implementing Data Protection*, is focused on data protection using the built-in support for encryption. If you want to prevent and minimize the consequences of data breaches, then this is the right chapter for you.

Chapter 10, *Indexing*, explains how to use different types of indexing to achieve better performance for your SQL code. The reader will learn how to recognize bottlenecks inside databases and apply the appropriate indexing methods.

Chapter 11, *In-Memory OLTP*, shows the readers how to implement different types of in-memory OLTP features.

Chapter 12, *Beyond SQL Server*, takes you on a beautiful journey through the rest of the features and tools that can be used in SQL Server development.

What you need for this book

This book is a highly practical guide for SQL Server on Linux. We focus on how to get things up-and-running, whether or not you have any prior SQL Server or Linux experience. To achieve the full potential and get the maximum benefits from this book, you will need one of these Linux distributions: Ubuntu 16.04 or Ubuntu 17.04, openSUSE Leap 42.2 or openSUSE Tumbleweed, Kubuntu 16.04 or 17.04, Red Hat Enterprise Linux 7.3, SUSE, or Linux Enterprise Server v12 SP2.
Last but not least, you will need to install SQL Server on Linux. At the time of writing, the last actual version was SQL Server on Linux RC1. I recommend the Developer edition. We have tried to keep all the code as user-friendly and readable as possible. We feel that this will enable our readers to easily understand it, and readily use it, in different scenarios.

Who this book is for

This book is for the Linux users who want to learn SQL Server on their favorite Linux distributions. It is not important if you are experienced database user or a beginner as we are starting from scratch. However, it is recommended that you have basic knowledge about relational models. More advanced readers can pick the chapters of their interest and study specific topics immediately. Users from Windows platform can also benefit from this book to expand their frontiers and become equally efficient on both platforms..

Conventions

In this book, you will find a number of text styles that distinguish between different kinds of information. Here are some examples of these styles and an explanation of their meaning. Code words in text, database table names, folder names, filenames, file extensions, pathnames, dummy URLs, user input, and Twitter handles are shown as follows: "Execute the following SELECT statement and count the number of records."

Any command-line input or output is written as follows:

```
1> ALTER DATABASE CURRENT
2> SET COMPATIBILITY_LEVEL = 130;
3> GO
```

New terms and **important words** are shown in bold. Words that you see on the screen, for example, in menus or dialog boxes, appear in the text like this: "In order to download new modules, we will go to **Files | Settings | Project Name | Project Interpreter**."

Warnings or important notes appear like this.

Tips and tricks appear like this.

Reader feedback

Feedback from our readers is always welcome. Let us know what you think about this book-what you liked or disliked. Reader feedback is important for us as it helps us develop titles that you will really get the most out of. To send us general feedback, simply e-mail feedback@packtpub.com, and mention the book's title in the subject of your message. If there is a topic that you have expertise in and you are interested in either writing or contributing to a book, see our author guide at www.packtpub.com/authors.

Customer support

Now that you are the proud owner of a Packt book, we have a number of things to help you to get the most from your purchase.

Downloading the example code

You can download the example code files for this book from your account at http://www.p acktpub.com. If you purchased this book elsewhere, you can visit www.packtpub.com/support and register to have the files e-mailed directly to you. You can download the code files by following these steps:

1. Log in or register to our website using your e-mail address and password.
2. Hover the mouse pointer on the **SUPPORT** tab at the top.
3. Click on **Code Downloads & Errata**.
4. Enter the name of the book in the **Search** box.
5. Select the book for which you're looking to download the code files.
6. Choose from the drop-down menu where you purchased this book from.
7. Click on **Code Download**.

Once the file is downloaded, please make sure that you unzip or extract the folder using the latest version of:

- WinRAR / 7-Zip for Windows
- Zipeg / iZip / UnRarX for Mac
- 7-Zip / PeaZip for Linux

The code bundle for the book is also hosted on GitHub at https://github.com/PacktPubl ishing/SQL-Server-on-Linux. We also have other code bundles from our rich catalog of books and videos available at https://github.com/PacktPublishing/. Check them out!

Errata

Although we have taken every care to ensure the accuracy of our content, mistakes do happen. If you find a mistake in one of our books-maybe a mistake in the text or the code-we would be grateful if you could report this to us. By doing so, you can save other readers from frustration and help us improve subsequent versions of this book. If you find any errata, please report them by visiting www.packtpub.com/submit-errata, selecting your book, clicking on the **Errata Submission Form** link, and entering the details of your errata. Once your errata are verified, your submission will be accepted and the errata will be uploaded to our website or added to any list of existing errata under the Errata section of that title. To view the previously submitted errata, go to https://www.packtpub.com/books/content/supportand enter the name of the book in the search field. The required information will appear under the **Errata** section.

Piracy

Piracy of copyrighted material on the Internet is an ongoing problem across all media. At Packt, we take the protection of our copyright and licenses very seriously. If you come across any illegal copies of our works in any form on the Internet, please provide us with the location address or website name immediately so that we can pursue a remedy. Please contact us at copyright@packtpub.com with a link to the suspected pirated material. We appreciate your help in protecting our authors and our ability to bring you valuable content.

Questions

If you have a problem with any aspect of this book, you can contact us at questions@packtpub.com, and we will do our best to address the problem.

1
Linux Distributions

Welcome to the exciting new journey of our old friend in a new environment. Yes, we are talking about one of the best database platforms in the world. SQL Server is well known in the domain of the Windows operating system, whether we speak of small, medium, or enterprise-size businesses. Cloud computing pushes those limits even further in the directions of big data analytics and data science. SQL Server has it all.

Linux, or to be precise GNU/Linux, is one of the best alternatives to Windows and, in many cases, it is the first choice of environment for daily tasks such as system administration, running different kinds of services, or just a tool for desktop application. Linux, which is the actual name for a kernel, was originally developed in 1991 by Linus Torvalds as his response to the MINIX operating system, which was limited to educational use. It was quickly recognized by the open source community, adopted, and packaged in many distributions. It's fascinating how large that number is. I believe that you've heard or read at least one name in the following list (the list is arranged by date (1993 - 2013)): Debian, Slackware, SUSE Linux, Red Hat Linux, CentOS, Fedora, Ubuntu, Tails, Kali Linux, and many more. Today, GNU/Linux does not hold a large chunk of the desktop operating system market. That fact is changing and many people, organizations, businesses, and even states are embracing this technology. But, if we talk about the server market, the situation is quite the opposite. Linux is holding a large share of the market.

However, Linux territory was a no-go for Microsoft products for a long time to be precise, from the beginning. Now, Microsoft loves Linux. A couple of years ago, this sentence would've sounded like a bad science fiction scenario. Fortunately, Microsoft has changed and become friendly to open source and free software philosophies. One of the reasons for this 180 degree change is cloud computing. New paradigms simply don't push old platform limitations to the background. Everything is a service now and it is not important where that service (Windows/Linux/Unix) is. The fact that Microsoft is pushing its core product on a couple of major Linux distributions speaks for itself.

However, one segment of the database ecosystem was out of Microsoft's reach. Linux was mostly reserved for open source representatives such as MySQL, PostgreSQL, and MariaDB, or proprietary ones such as IBM's DB2 and Oracle. But now it is time to change those facts. We can say that Microsoft is officially offering their data platform flagship as options and choice for database professionals in the Linux world. There are varied kinds of responses to this subject, from totally negative to positive comments. My opinion is that this is good thing. SQL Server is one of the best database environments; let's give them a chance to prove it on the ground. The Linux ecosystem has become richer and end users have more choices to pick the right solution for their needs.

This is not a book about Linux distributions, nor is it about Linux internals. Here, you will not find any Linux command line reference, but you will find a lot of useful information on how to deal with SQL Server on Linux.

This chapter targets DBAs, developers, and everyone else from the Windows playground. If you are from this group of users and you want to try out SQL Server in Linux land but don't know how to start, this is the chapter for you. If you are a Linux user with experience in your favorite distribution or different kinds of distributions, you can skip this chapter and go straight to the installation part.

In this chapter we will cover the following topics:

- Supported Linux distributions
- Installation of Linux operating system

Supported Linux distributions

When this book was written, SQL Server on Linux supported all major distributions:

- **Commercial**: Red Hat Enterprise Linux 7.3 Workstation, Server, and Desktop
- **Commercial**: SUSE Enterprise Linux Server v12 SP2
- **Free**: Ubuntu 16.04 LTS and 16.10

Red Hat Enterprise Linux and SUSE Enterprise Linux are commercial versions of popular open source and free distributions. So, this list can be easily expanded to include the following distributions:

- openSUSE Leap/Tumbleweed
- Fedora

The two are not officially listed in the documentation but they work just fine, the same as the commercial versions. If you don't have any Linux experience whatsoever, I recommend Ubuntu or openSUSE. These two distributions will be covered in this chapter, specifically how to install them and prepare for SQL Server installation.

openSUSE

This distribution has a long history (`https://www.suse.com/company/history/`). The journey started under the name of SUSE Linux in 1994. Later, in 2003, Novel bought SUSE and its brand and trademark. The company recognized the importance of the community and created openSUSE, preserving the open source philosophy.

Novel was acquired by The Attachmate Group in 2011 and SUSE became an independent part of the company business. In a nutshell, SUSE has two product lines:

- **Commercial**: **SUSE Enterprise Server** (**SLES**)
- **openSUSE**: an independent community project based on SLES source code

Microsoft officially supports SLES, but openSUSE is in that train also.

Installation procedure

Let's start with the installation of openSUSE Leap 42.2, stable release. I will use a Hyper-V virtualization environment, but any other, such as VMWare or Oracle Virtual Box, will be just fine. If you are planning to install a native Linux environment without virtualization, the steps are the same. The installation of ISO can be found at `https://www.opensuse.org/`. You can mount ISO directly inside your virtual machine, create a bootable USB drive, or burn a DVD. The choice is yours.

The steps for the installation of openSUSE Leap 42.2 are as follows:

1. The welcome screen will show up after the initial boot procedure from USB drive, DVD ROM, or ISO image directly as shown in the following screenshot.

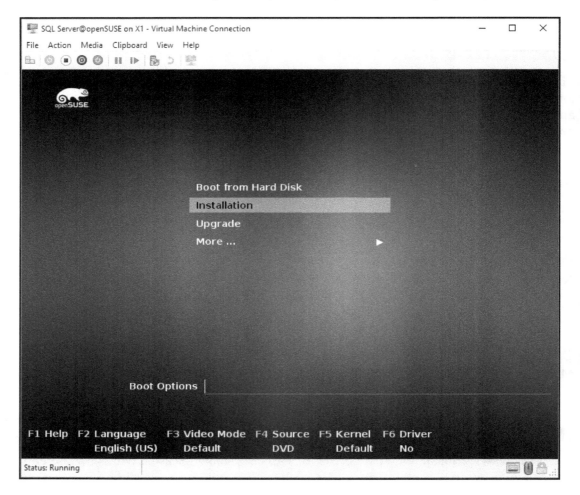

Figure 1-1. openSUSE welcome screen

2. In the next step, you can choose to book from the hard drive, start a fresh installation of openSUSE, run an upgrade process of an old installation, or initialize some advanced steps. We will choose **Installation**.

3. Now, we pick the installation language and keyboard layout as shown in the following screenshot. You can test specific language characters if you come from non-English region. The license agreement is also there. Click **Next** after you are satisfied with your choices.

Figure 1-2. Keyboard layout and license agreement

4. Linux can work without a network connection, but for full efficiency, this step is recommended. Here you will see a list of all network adapters that are recognized by the setup procedure in your PC, laptop, or virtual machine.

You can click on **Next** and finish network configuration after the installation procedure (if you decide to configure the network after installation, skip to the disk partition creation part), or you can do it now by choosing the network adapter name and clicking on **Edit**.

In most use cases, choosing **Dynamic Address** will be just fine. It will give you IP address, DNS, and Gateway settings. However, in some situations, you will need to manually enter those parameters by selecting **Statically Assigned IP Address** (In this scenario, you will need to know the DNS setting and gateway parameters to successfully configure network settings manually)

This is an important step if you are planning to use internet access in the following steps.

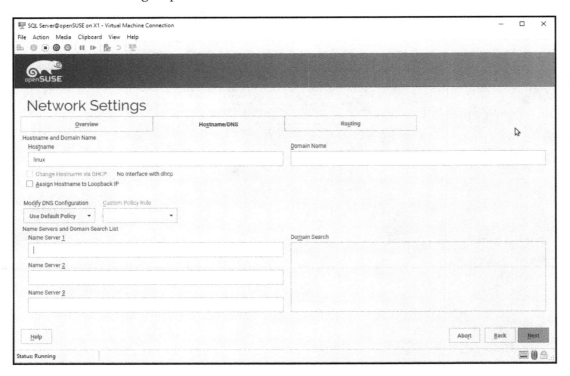

Figure 1-3. Set up the network

5. openSUSE comes with a huge collection of software and an excellent built-in package manager, but still you can install a lot more from separate media. Also you can add online software repositories before the installation starts. If you choose online repositories, then you will need an internet connection (you can go back to configure it, or you can leave both options off and activate those options after installation).

A slow internet connection can slow down your installation and you will need separate installation media for the add-ons. If you are an inexperienced Linux user, then I suggest that you leave the network connection and online repositories configuration until after installation is done.

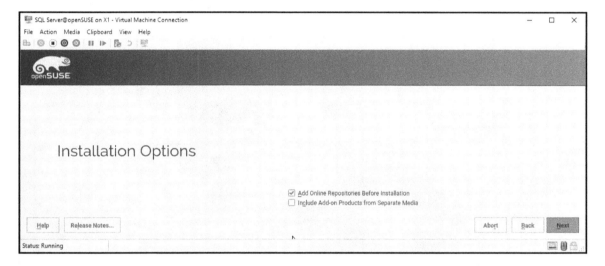

Figure 1-4. Option to add online repositories during install

6. You have the option to add online repositories during this step, you can choose your region and corresponding time zone. The same as in a Windows environment, these settings are reflecting the latter in the operating system and application that are depended on these parameters. The GUI is very nice, and by simply clicking, you can zoom in and focus on your country. By clicking on **Other Settings**, you can fine-tune those settings.

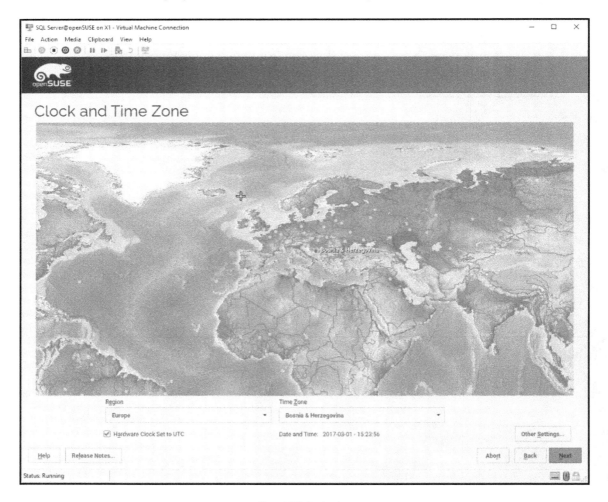

Figure 1-5. Regional settings

7. Now is the moment of truth. Yes, seriously. This step will adapt your frontend and install the desktop environment of your choice.

Figure 1-6. Desktop selection

Almost every Linux distribution gives you two options. When it comes to openSUSE, you can pick one of the following:

- KDE Plasma desktop (`https://www.kde.org/`)
- GNOME desktop (`https://www.gnome.org/`)
- Server (text mode)
- Other

Let us take a look at each one:

- **KDE Plasma desktop**: KDE is not something new on the scene. It has been here since 1996 and in more than 20 years it has built a loyal user base. It is simple, efficient, robust, and Windows-like. You even have a **Start** (K) menu. If you are coming from a Windows background, then this should be your first choice. Don't get me wrong! KDE is popular in the world of Linux distributions. KDE is also my first choice and I will use it as the default installation option for openSUSE and Kubuntu (the KDE version of Ubuntu).
- **GNOME desktop**: It is same as in the example before, GNOME is on the stage since 1999 and the user base is also large. We can say that the Linux community is divided between KDE and GNOME desktop environments. This is not a bad thing. Differences and options are good things and, if you are not a **Start** menu fan, then GNOME is just for you. openSUSE distribution comes with KDE as the default.

- **Server** (text mode): This mode is simple, fast, and a good old Command Prompt environment. If you are planning to run some kind of production service (web, mail, FTP, and so on), there is no need for GUI at all (this philosophy is taken and implemented in Windows OS (Windows Core and Nano version)).

Figure 1-7. Creating initial local user

1. The next step is about creating new user profile for daily tasks. Unlike Windows, Linux does not have admin first philosophy. This is regular user without root (super user permissions). It is not a good idea to work neater on Windows or Linux as admin (root). If you check **Use this password for system administrator**, the same password will be associated with root account. It will be required for admin tasks. However, if you skip this option it will bring you to the next screen where you can define different root password. This step is so important that installation gives you an option to test the keyboard layout just in case you are planning to use some exotic kind of characters.

Figure 1-8. Password for root access

2. The next step is reviewing of chosen options. Still, you can go back and correct/modify some parameters before changes become permanent. After some time, when setup finishes you will get login screen. Enter your credentials and you are ready to go with openSUSE.

This book is not an openSUSE user guide, so if you are Windows user then you can reference some additional resources, but it will be easy. KDE is something familiar and its GUI is efficient enough to support your exploring through this great distribution.

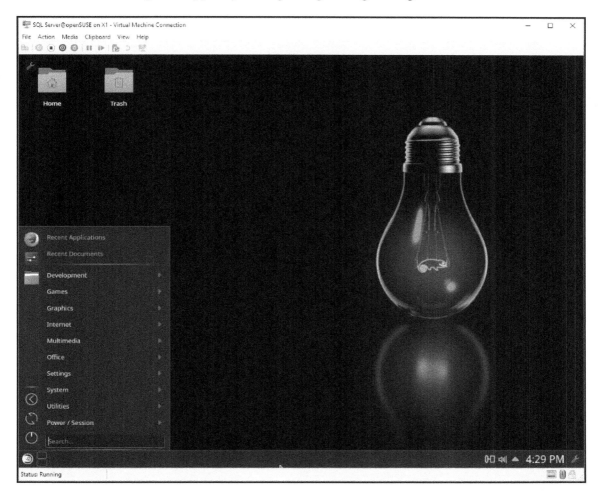

Figure 1-9. Welcome to openSUSE

Kubuntu

Ubuntu is one of the simplest and most user friendly Linux distributions. It's based on Debian like many other distros whose roots date back to the distant 2004. Ubuntu is, by default, a GNOME (Unity) based environment which is OK. But my opinion is that Windows users will find it a little bit confusing. KDE is much better for them. Kubuntu is official flavor of the Ubuntu based on KDE plasma desktop, started in 2005. From the perspective of SQL Server there is no difference at all because most of our work will be console based.

Installation procedure

Kubuntu has a different approach than openSUSE. At the same time, Kubuntu is a live distribution, it means that after boot you are directly in the working environment where you can test things. At any time, you can start installation and make permanent changes on your disk. This following screenshot shows how Kubuntu looks after boot procedure.

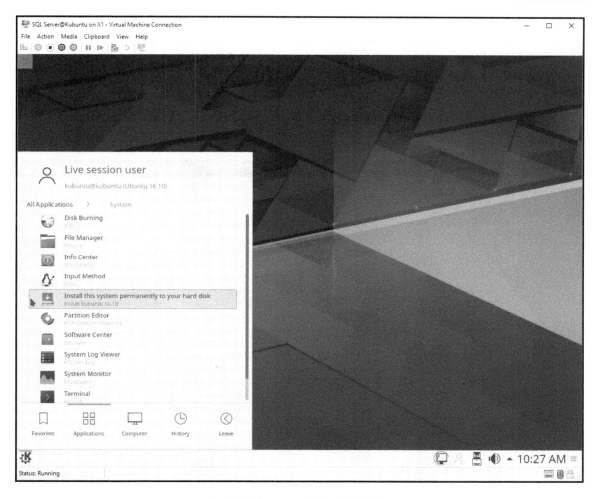

Figure 1-10. Welcome screen of Kubuntu live distribution

If you are not an adventurous type and you like to keep things simple, then Kubuntu is your kind of Linux distribution.

Now, you can test the environment by running different kinds of applications: Libre Office, Firefox, Thunderbird, GIMP, and so on, or you can click on **K menu** | **Applications** | **System** | **Install this system permanently to hard disk**. After this step, the process of Kubuntu installation is very similar to openSUSE. The installation procedure involves the following steps:

1. First, you need to choose the language for the install process and it will be the default language for that computer.

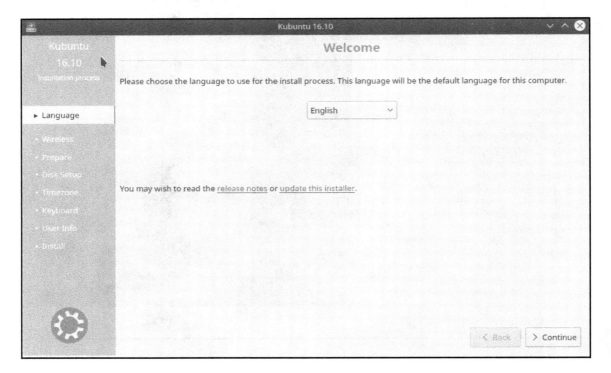

Figure 1-11. Language settings

2. The next step is to configure network connection. During the testing phase, before installation, you can make right click on the icon of the screen near to the clock and setup you network parameters. Those setting are recognized by the setup procedure and used later.

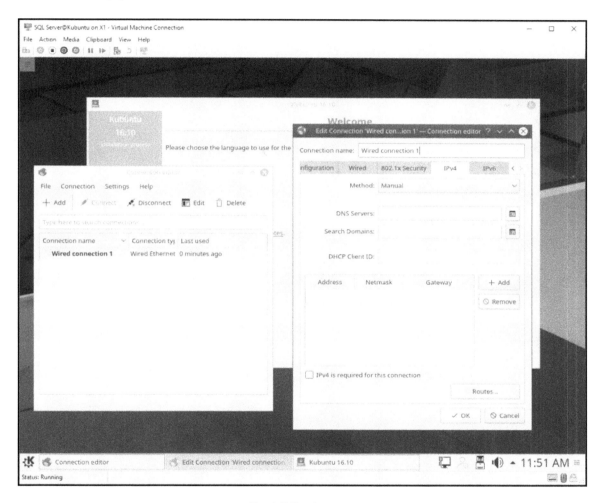

Figure 1-12. Network parameters

3. If the network is working, then you can download updates while installing Kubuntu and/or install third party software. You can skip this step and finish it later.

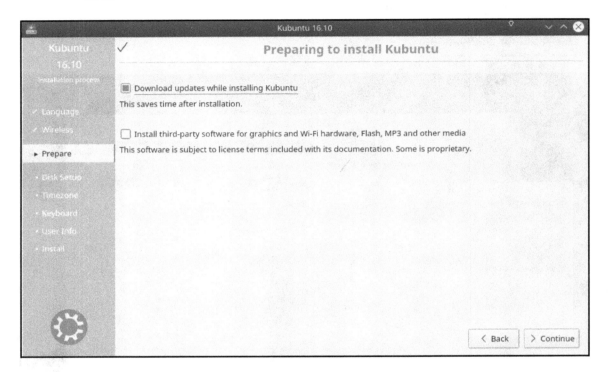

Figure 1-13. Option to add online repositories during install

4. We must be honest and admit Kubuntu is much simpler to install the openSUSE. One of the proofs is disk setup. All you need is to pick an option without necessary technical details. Those details can scare users who don't have experience with disk partitioning. We can apply the same rule as before. If you're just starting with Linux and you don't care about the partitioning thing, then you chose **Guided - use entire disk**. After this step, changes on the disk become permanent and it may lead to data loss.

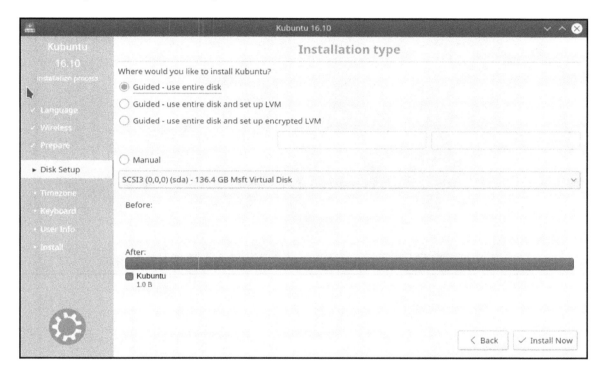

Figure 1-14. Disk partitioning

5. Now, you need to select your location and time zone settings is next step. This is important because of the display conventions for your country.

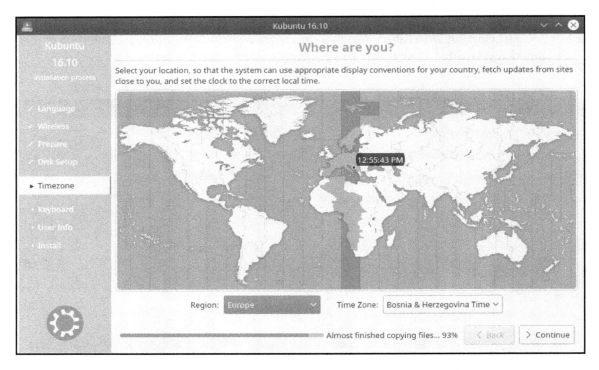

Figure 1-15. Regional settings

6. This leads to a screen where you can choose a keyboard layout and variant, if any. The nice thing is that you can actually see specific language letters and compare them with your physical keyboard.

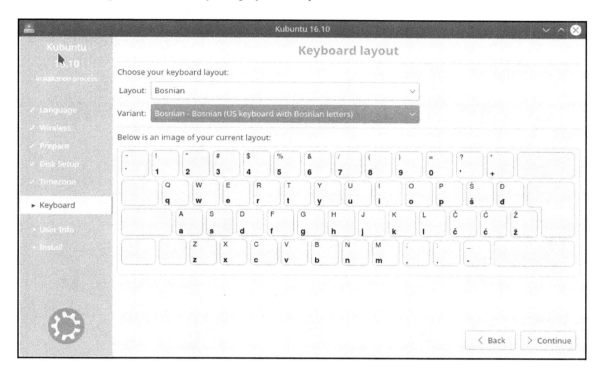

Figure 1-16. Choosing and testing the keyboard layout

7. The last step before your setup finishes is to choose your credentials: username, password, and computer name. Kubuntu will not give you an option to choose a root password. It can be done later. Actually, there is no need to use root at all. For that purpose, there is a program called **sudo**. It allows you to run programs with the security privileges of another user. The default is super user. On Kubuntu, calling the su command will require you to enter your account password to execute the command, which requires super user privileges. Setup will add your username to the sudo group.

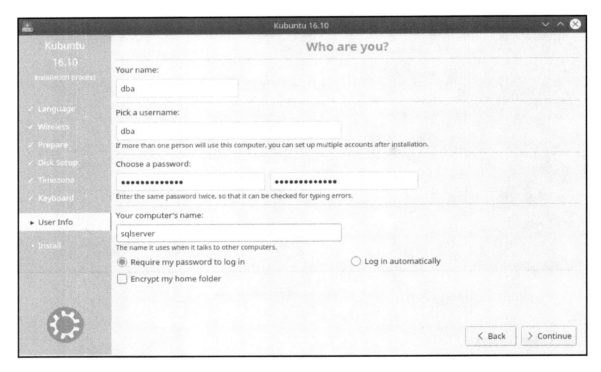

Figure 1-17. Creating the initial local user

Summary

In this chapter, you learned the basics of Linux and how SQL Server has become part of this story. After that, we explained what Linux is and how to install one of the two popular distributions, both supported by SQL Server on Linux. Now, after the initial steps on your working/learning environment, we can dig a little bit deeper. In the next chapter we will see how to install SQL Server on openSUSE, downloading Linux packages and initial security settings.

2
Installation and Configuration

Linux's native working interface is the command line. Yes, KDE and GNOME are great graphic user interfaces however from a user's perspective, clicking is much easier than typing, but this observation is relative. Many Linux and Windows users will disagree with me; I am somewhere in the middle. GUI is something that changed the perception of modern IT and computer usage. Some tasks are very difficult without a mouse, but not impossible.

On the other hand, command line is something where you can solve some tasks quicker, more efficiently, and better than in GUI. You don't believe me? Imagine these situations and try to implement them through your favorite GUI tool:

- From a folder of 1,000 files, copy only those which names start with letter A, end with letter Z, and end with TXT extension
- Rename 100 files at the same time
- Redirect console output to the file

There are many such examples; in each of them, command prompt is superior--Linux bash, even more so.

 The first part of this chapter, *Bash, really quick start* is for Windows users with very little or no command line experience. If you are a Linux user, you can safely skip to the installation section.

In this chapter we will cover the following topics:

- SQL Server installation on openSUSE
- SQL Server installation on Kubuntu
- Initial security settings

Bash, really quick start

Linux bash is going way beyond the scope of this book, but I will cover basic commands, which you may need in your daily work with SQL Server on Linux, such as creating folders, copying files, navigating through a tree of folders, deleting files and folders, listing content of folders and current position in the folder tree.

- pwd
- ls
- cd
- mkdir
- cp
- rm
- rmdir

You can run the command line bash tool in many ways. Here, you can find two of the most common ways. Assuming that you have a KDE environment, click on **K menu | System | Konsole**.

Alternately, press *Alt+Space* and start typing Konsole. You will see at the top of the screen a menu with a list of tools, programs, files, and everything else that has the word **Konsole** in the name. Just choose **Konsole Terminal** as shown in the following screenshot and press *Enter*:

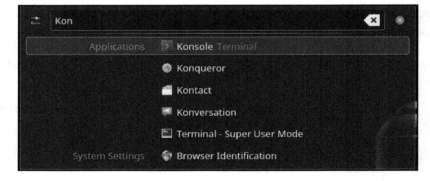

Figure 2-1. Choosing **Konsole Terminal** option to run bash

After you run the **Konsole Terminal** bash application, depending on the version of Linux, username, and host name, you should see something like this:

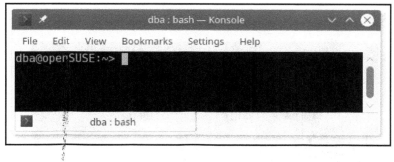

Figure 2-2. Command prompt in bash Konsole

The current location is your Home directory, which is your username.

How do you check what your current position on the directory tree is? The Linux command for this kind of a job is pwd. If you type pwd and press *Enter*, bash will show your current position on the filesystem, as you can see in the following screenshot:

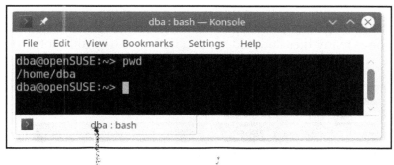

Figure 2-3. Effect of pwd command

My current position is /home/dba. The first forward slash is the root directory. It means that home is subdirectory of root.

I believe many of you are familiar with the old DOS command (Windows as well): `dir`. The Linux equivalent is `ls`. Take a look at the next screenshot:

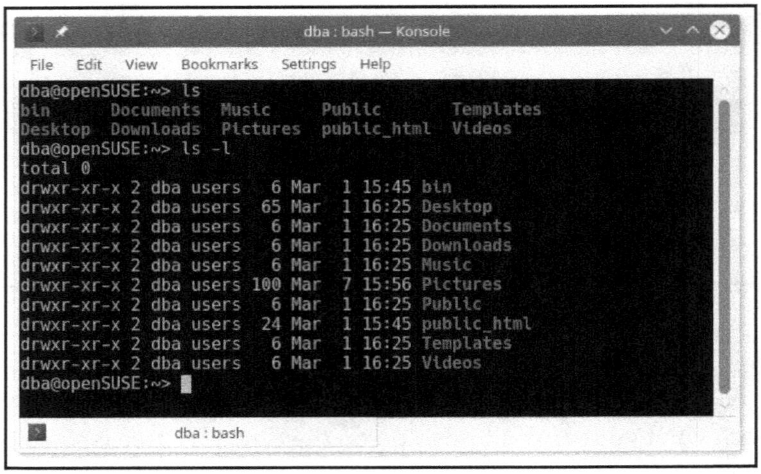

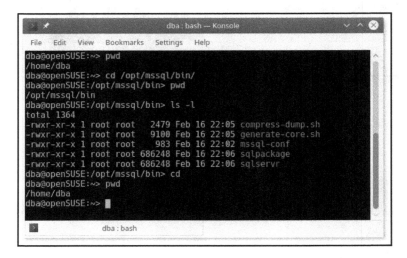

Figure 2-4. Result of ls command without and with parameter -l

When you type just `ls` without any argument and parameters, it gives you a list of files and folders. The output is not descriptive. But, if you type `ls  -l`, the output is much better. In this case, if you have many files and folders, you will need to scroll a lot; so the first option is better:

Figure 2-5. Combination of different bash commands

The scenario from figure 2-5 can be summarized as follows:

1. Check your current position with the pwd command.

   dba@openSUSE:~> pwd

2. Change the path from home/dba to: /opt/mssql/bin/ with the cd command.

   dba@openSUSE:~> cd /opt/mssql/bin/

3. Again, check the current position.

   dba@openSUSE:~> pwd

4. List the content /opt/mssql/bin/ folder with the ls -l command.

   dba@openSUSE:~> ls -l

5. Go back to home/dba with a single cd command and check your new position with pwd.

   dba@openSUSE:~> cd

The next scenario will combine all commands from previous cases with the addition of: creating new folders, copying, and removing files. First, take a look at the following screenshot:

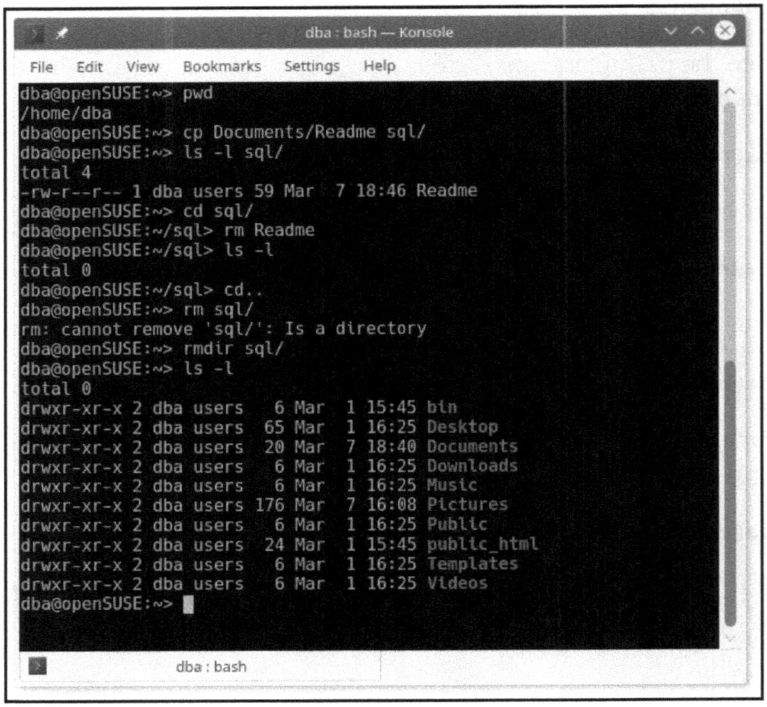

Figure 2-6. Working with files and folders trough bash

The scenario from figure 2-6 can be summarized as follows:

1. Check your current position with the pwd command.

   ```
   dba@openSUSE:~> pwd
   ```

2. With the cp command, you will copy the Readme file from the Documents folder to the sql folder. Both folders are on same level, as sub-folders of home/dba (in my case).

   ```
   dba@openSUSE:~> cp Documents/Readme sql/
   ```

3. Change the path from home to `sql/` with the cd command.

```
dba@openSUSE:~> cd sql/
```

4. Delete the `Readme` file from the `sql/` folder with the rm command:

```
dba@openSUSE:~> rm Readme
```

5. List the `content sql/` folder with the `ls -l` command. As you see, the total number of files is 0 because we just deleted `Readme`.

```
dba@openSUSE:~> ls -l
```

6. This takes you back to `home/dba` with the cd command (only one level in the tree, from `sql` to `dba`).

```
dba@openSUSE:~> cd..
```

7. You can't delete folders with the rm command.

```
dba@openSUSE:~> rm sql/
```

8. You can delete folders with the `rmdir` command.

```
dba@openSUSE:~> rmdir sql/
```

9. List the content `home/dba` folder with the `ls -l` command. As you see, the `sql` subfolder is gone from the the list files.

```
dba@openSUSE:~> ls -l
```

This quick bash introduction will be enough to start interacting with Linux through the command line interface. You will need some of these commands later in the book to finish some tasks, such as creating backup folders, copying database backups, modifying SQL scripts, and so on. If you would like to learn more about command line on Linux, I would recommend additional reading *The Linux Command Line*, a book by William Shotts.

 If you are planning to commit yourself to some serious database administration on SQL Server or any other database platform, then bash is something that you will use most of the time. I strongly advice that you invest your time in this area.

SQL Server installation on openSUSE

The following installation procedure is the same for the SUSE Linux Enterprise Server v12 SP2 (SLES), which is officially supported by the Microsoft Corporation. My example is based on openSUSE Leap 42.2.

Another remark is that the installation is based on the SQL Server vNext CTP 1.3 RC1 set of versions, which were actual at the time of writing this book. The installation procedure is command line-based. It means that you will be required to use bash. openSUSE and Kubuntu use the same bash client, Konsole.

 If you want to start installation on openSUSE or SLES, you will need minimum 3.25GB of memory to run the SQL Server on Linux. The file system must be XFS or EXT4.

Following are the steps to install SQL Server on Linux on openSUSE:

1. First of all, you will need to add the `mssql-server` package to your distribution with the following two commands as shown in the screenshot:

   ```
   # sudo zypper addrepo -fc
   https://packages.microsoft.com/config/sles/12/mssql-server.repo
   # sudo zypper --gpg-auto-import-keys refresh
   ```

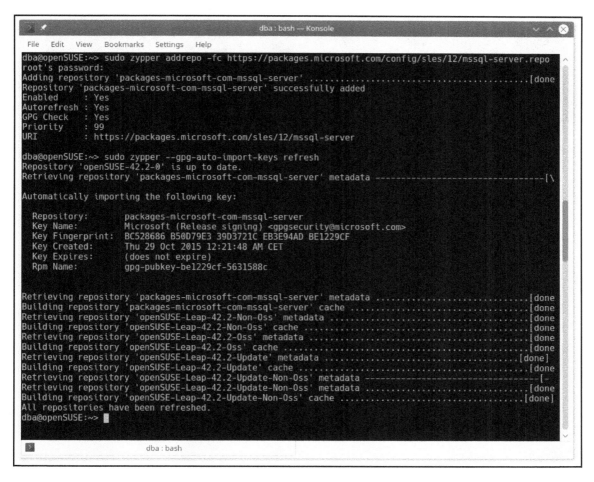

Figure 2-7. Result of adding msql-server packages

2. Now openSUSE knows where to look and find SQL Server binaries. Installation can start with this command:

```
# sudo zypper install mssql-server
```

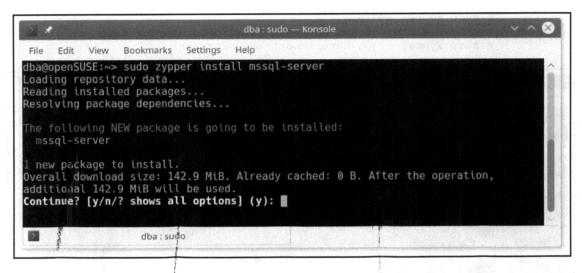

```
dba : sudo — Konsole

File   Edit   View   Bookmarks   Settings   Help

dba@openSUSE:~> sudo zypper install mssql-server
Loading repository data...
Reading installed packages...
Resolving package dependencies...

The following NEW package is going to be installed:
  mssql-server

1 new package to install.
Overall download size: 142.9 MiB. Already cached: 0 B. After the operation,
additional 142.9 MiB will be used.
Continue? [y/n/? shows all options] (y):

dba : sudo
```

Figure 2-8. Result of step two should be like this. Press *y* or *n* to start/abort this process

3. After the installation is over, you can run the `mssql-conf` setup and follow the procedure. For the sake of security, you need to specify a strong password for the **sa** account (**system administrator**). The minimum length is eight characters, a combination of uppercase and lowercase letters, 10 digits and/or non-alphanumeric symbols:

```
# sudo /opt/mssql/bin/mssql-conf setup
```

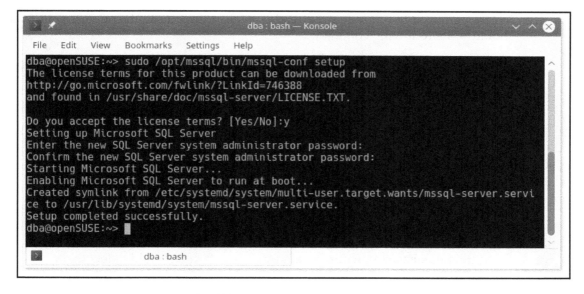

Figure 2-9. Setting up sa account and finishing install procedure

4. Now is the time to check the status of the SQL Server service:

```
# systemctl status mssql-server
```

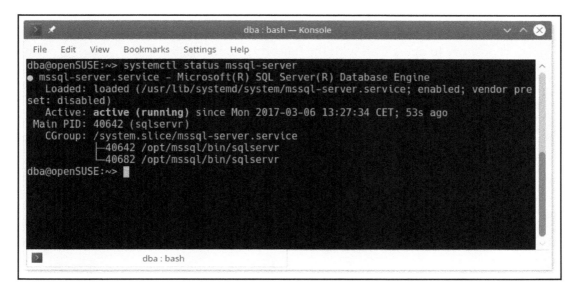

Figure 2-10. Information that SQL Server database engine is up and running

5. In case you need to upgrade the already installed binaries to the new version, you should write following command:

```
# sudo zypper update mssql-server
```

6. If you wish to remove the SQL Server from your Linux distribution, write the next bash command:

```
# sudo zypper remove mssql-server
```

So, SQL Server is successfully installed, and service is up and running. The next step is the installation procedure for `mssql-tools` repository. It is set of a client (command line) applications to interact with database engine.

 The upgrade process will not affect the user and system databases that are located in `/opt/mssql/`. On the other hand, *step 6* will not delete user and system database located in: `/var/opt/mssql`; you should delete them manually.

SQL Server for Linux in this phase of development has only command line-tools. We are speaking in terms of the Linux platform. The original SQL Server Management Studio, built for Windows, can be used to work with SQL Server on Linux. The only catch is that you need Windows side by side or as a remote client. This book is dealing with Linux, so the focus will be on command line access.

1. As in the first step of engine installation, we need to add the `mssql-tools` repository to openSUSE with the following commands:

```
# sudo zypper addrepo -fc
https://packages.microsoft.com/config/sles/12/prod.repo
# sudo zypper --gpg-auto-import-keys refresh
```

2. To install `mssql-tools` with the necessary `unixODBC` developer package, type the following command:

```
# sudo zypper install mssql-tools unixODBC-devel
```

3. The following screenshot illustrates the process of installing the tools component. After you say yes, you will be asked to accept (or not) the licence agreement. If you decide to say no, the installation will stop:

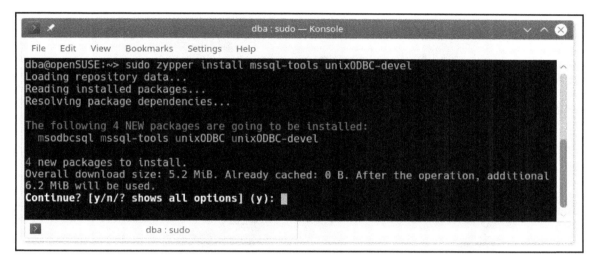

Figure 2-11. Starting installation of mssql-tools

4. In case you want to update only tools to the new version, you run these two commands:

```
# sudo zypper refresh
# sudo zypper update mssql-tools
```

5. The next step is optional and can save you a lot of time initially while you figure out what is going on. At this moment, bash does not know where the `mssql-tools` repository is, so you will need to modify your `PATH` environment variable. The following two commands are referenced for running the `sqlcmd` and `bpc` command-line tools:

```
# echo 'export PATH="$PATH:/opt/mssql-tools/bin"'>> ~/.bash_profile
# echo 'export PATH="$PATH:/opt/mssql-tools/bin"' >> ~/.bashrc
# source ~/.bashrc
```

6. Now you need to test your tool. The only way to do this is to try to connect on SQL Server database engine. To start, just type the following:

```
# sqlcmd
```

7. If you see something like the following screenshot, then you are on the right path:

```
                            dba : bash — Konsole

  File   Edit   View   Bookmarks   Settings   Help
dba@openSUSE:~> sqlcmd
Microsoft (R) SQL Server Command Line Tool
Version 13.1.0001.0 Linux
Copyright (c) 2012 Microsoft. All rights reserved.

usage: sqlcmd            [-U login id]           [-P password]
  [-S server or Dsn if -D is provided]
  [-H hostname]              [-E trusted connection]
  [-N Encrypt Connection][-C Trust Server Certificate]
  [-d use database name] [-l login timeout]    [-t query timeout]
  [-h headers]               [-s colseparator]    [-w screen width]
  [-a packetsize]          [-e echo input]      [-I Enable Quoted Identifiers]
  [-c cmdend]
  [-q "cmdline query"]   [-Q "cmdline query" and exit]
  [-m errorlevel]          [-V severitylevel]    [-W remove trailing spaces]
  [-u unicode output]    [-r[0|1] msgs to stderr]
  [-i inputfile]            [-o outputfile]
  [-k[1|2] remove[replace] control characters]
  [-y variable length type display width]
  [-Y fixed length type display width]
  [-p[1] print statistics[colon format]]
  [-R use client regional setting]
  [-K application intent]
  [-M multisubnet failover]
  [-b On error batch abort]
  [-D Dsn flag, indicate -S is Dsn]
  [-X[1] disable commands, startup script, environment variables [and exit]]
  [-x disable variable substitution]
  [-? show syntax summary]
dba@openSUSE:~> ■

              dba : bash
```

Figure 2-12. Result of sqlcmd command

SQL Server installation on Kubuntu

The installation procedure on Kubuntu is identical to that in Ubuntu 16.04 and 16.10, which are officially supported by Microsoft. Kubuntu and Ubuntu share the same version numbering. My installation example is based on Kubuntu 16.10.

The whole installation procedure is command line-based. It means that you will be required to use bash.

 If you want to start installation, you will need minimum 3.25GB of memory to run SQL Server on Linux.

The following are the steps to install SQL Server on Linux on Kubuntu:

1. The first step is to add GPG keys and register SQL Server Ubuntu repository:

    ```
    # curl https://packages.microsoft.com/keys/microsoft.asc | sudo
    apt-key add -
    # curl
    https://packages.microsoft.com/config/ubuntu/16.04/mssql-server.list | sudo
    tee
    /etc/apt/sources.list.d/mssql-server.list
    ```

2. Run the following two commands to install SQL Server. The first one is to refresh the packages list and the second one to start setting up:

    ```
    # sudo apt-get update
    # sudo apt-get install -y mssql-server
    ```

3. After the installation is over, you can run the `mssql-conf` setup and follow the procedure. For the sake of security, you need to specify a strong password for the sa account. The minimum length is eight characters, a combination of uppercase and lowercase letters, 10 digits, and/or non-alphanumeric symbols:

    ```
    # sudo /opt/mssql/bin/mssql-conf setup
    ```

4. Now is the time to check the status of the SQL Server service:

    ```
    # systemctl status mssql-server
    ```

5. In case you need to upgrade the already installed binaries to the new version, you should write two commands. The first one is to refresh the packages list and the second one to start the upgrade procedure:

    ```
    # sudo apt-get update
    # sudo apt-get install mssql-server
    ```

6. If you wish to remove the SQL Server from your Linux distribution, write the next bash command:

    ```
    # sudo apt-get remove mssql-server
    ```

The upgrade process will not affect user and system databases that are located in /opt/mssql/. On the other hand, *step 6* will not delete user and system database located in: /var/opt/mssql; you should delete them manually.

7. Before installing the tool components, we need to import public GPG keys and register the Microsoft Ubuntu repository with the following commands:

```
# curl https://packages.microsoft.com/keys/microsoft.asc | sudo
apt-key add -
# curl https://packages.microsoft.com/config/ubuntu/16.04/prod.list
| sudo tee
/etc/apt/sources.list.d/msprod.list
```

8. To install `mssql-tools` with the necessary `unixODBC` developer package, type the following command:

```
# sudo apt-get update
# sudo apt-get install mssql-tools unixodbc-dev
```

9. In case you want to update only tools for the new version, run these two commands:

```
# sudo apt-get update
# sudo apt-get install mssql-tools
```

10. Now you will need to modify your `PATH` environment variable. The following two commands are referenced for running the `sqlcmd` and `bpc` command-line tools:

```
# echo 'export PATH="$PATH:/opt/mssql-tools/bin"' >>
~/.bash_profile
# echo 'export PATH="$PATH:/opt/mssql-tools/bin"' >> ~/.bashrc
# source ~/.bashrc
```

11. As in the openSUSE scenario, you need to test the client tools. You can type the same command:

```
# sqlcmd
```

Summary

In this chapter, you learned how to start interacting with Linux through the bash command-line utility. This is enough to finish all command line tasks that you will find in this book regarding SQL Server. A more detailed approach was on the installation procedure of SQL Server on Linux (openSUSE and Kubuntu distros).

In the next chapter, we'll take a look to the SQL Server architecture and some internals that are different compared with SQL Server on Windows.

3
SQL Server Basics

Microsoft SQL Server is considered to be one of the most commonly used systems for database management in the world. This popularity has been gained by a high degree of stability, security, and business intelligence and integration functionality. Microsoft SQL Server for Linux is a database server that accepts queries from clients, evaluates them, and then internally executes them to deliver results to the client. The client is an application that produces queries through a database provider and communication protocol sends requests to the server and retrieves the result for client-side processing and/or presentation.

Before starting to write queries and work with Microsoft SQL Server it's a good idea to gain a good understanding of how the software works. With a good understanding of the product and its mechanics, you'll be able to write more efficient queries and get results much faster.

In this chapter, we will cover the following topics:

- Overview of SQL Server
- SQL Server components
- How does it work on Linux?
- SQL Server objects
- SQL/T-SQL basics
- Working environments and tools

Overview of SQL Server

When writing queries, it's important to understand that the interaction between the tool of choice and the database based on client-server architecture, and the processes that are involved. It's also important to understand which components are available and what functionality they provide.

With a broader understanding of the full product and its components and tools, you'll be able to make better use of its functionality, and also benefit from using the right tool for specific jobs.

Client-server architecture concepts

In client-server architecture, the client is described as a user and/or device, and the server as a provider of some kind of service.

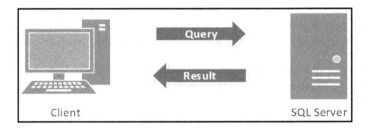

Figure 3-1. SQL Server client-server communication

As you can see in *Figure 3-1*, the client is represented as a machine, but in reality it can be anything:

- Custom application (desktop, mobile, web)
- Administration tool (SQL Server Management Studio, dbForge, sqlcmd)
- Development environment (Visual Studio, KDevelop)

SQL Server components

Microsoft SQL Server consists of many different components to serve a variety of organizational needs of their data platform. Some of these are:

- **Database Engine** is the relational database management system (RDBMS), which hosts databases and processes queries to return results of structured, semi-structured, and non-structured data in **online transactional processing solutions (OLTP)**.
- **Analysis Services** is the online analytical processing engine (OLAP) as well as the data mining engine. OLAP is a way of building multi-dimensional data structures for fast and dynamic analysis of large amounts of data, allowing users to navigate hierarchies and dimensions to reach granular and aggregated results to achieve a comprehensive understanding of business values. Data mining is a set of tools used to predict and analyze trends in data behavior and much more.
- **Integration Services** supports the need to extract data from sources, transform it, and load it in destinations (ETL) by providing a central platform that distributes and adjusts large amounts of data between heterogeneous data destinations.
- **Reporting Services** is a central platform for delivery of structured data reports and offers a standardized, universal data model for information workers to retrieve data and model reports without the need of understanding the underlying data structures.
- **Data Quality Services** (**DQS**) is used to perform a variety of data cleaning, correction, and data quality tasks, based on knowledge base. DQS is mostly used in ETL process before loading DW.
- **Machine Learning Services** (advanced analytics) is a new service that actually incorporates powerful R and Python languages for advanced statistic analytics. It is part of a database engine and you can combine classic SQL code with R and Python scripts.

 While writing this book, only one service was actually available in SQL Server for Linux and its database engine. This will change in the future and you can expect more services to be available.

How it works on Linux

SQL Server is a product with a 30 years long history of development. We are speaking about millions of lines of code on a single operating system (Windows). The logical question is how Microsoft successfully ports those millions of lines of code to the Linux platform so fast. SQL Server on Linux officially became public in the autumn of 2016. This process would take years of development and investment. Fortunately, it was not so hard.

From version 2005, the SQL Server database engine had a platform layer called **SQL operating system** (**SOS**). It is a layer between the SQL Server engine and the Windows operating systems.

The main purpose of SOS is to minimize the number of system calls by letting SQL Server deal with its own resources. It greatly improves performance, stability, and the debugging process. On the other hand, it is platform dependent and does not provide an abstraction layer. That was the first big problem encountered before even beginning to think about creating the Linux version.

Project Drawbridge is a Microsoft research project that was created to minimize virtualization resources when a host runs many VM on the same physical machine. The technical explanation goes beyond the scope of this book (https://www.microsoft.com/en-us/research/project/drawbridge/). Drawbridge bring us to the solution of the problem.

Linux solutions use a hybrid approach that combines SOS and Liberty OS from the Drawbridge project to create **SQL PAL** (**SQL Platform Abstraction Layer**). This approach creates a set of SOS API calls that does not require Win32 or NT calls and separates them from platform depended code. This is a dramatically reduced process of rewriting SQL Server from its native environment to Linux platform. The next figure gives you a high level overview of SQL PAL (https://blogs.technet.microsoft.com/dataplatforminsider/2016/12/16/sql-server-on-linux-how-introduction/):

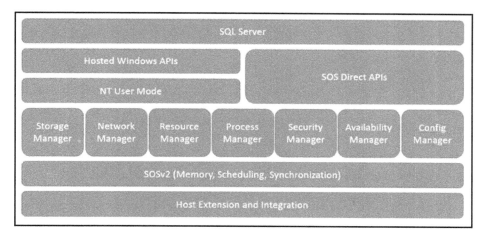

Figure 3-2. SQL PAL architecture.

SQL Server objects

In the following lines, we will present the basic structure of SQL Server objects, from the server to the database level. This book does not have the scope to cover all the elements of which we are going to speak, but it will give you enough information to cover all the basics.

System databases

SQL server has a concept of system and user databases. User databases are created for specific types of business process: HR, online shop, eHealth, and so on. It's up to the user (developers and DBAs) to define all the parameters. Here, you are in charge (more about it Chapter 4, *Database in the Sandbox*).

On the other hand, system databases are created during the installation procedure without almost any user influence. It is a repository of all SQL Server internals and it continues its process of updating its content, such as:

- Configuration data
- Users information
- Database objects

- Query execution statistics
- Troubleshooting
- Data statistics
- And many more

SQL Server simply can't work without it. All this important information is stored in the following system databases:

- `master` (system-wide settings and information about user databases)
- `tempdb` (a place for any temporal database tasks)
- `model` (the template for new user databases)
- `msdb` (used by SQL Server Agent Service for tasks scheduling)

Those four databases are default and the user can't directly access their content. To do that we need to use system catalog and dynamic management views objects.

Database objects

Tables are the containers for database records. They represent basic elements of the database structure. For example, `Students`, `Educators`, `Courses`, and `Grades` can be a table in some hypothetical eUniversity system. Tables are built around data types bounded on table columns. For example, `LastName - nvarchar(50)`, `Salary - Money`, `BirthDate - datetime`. Every data operation includes tables and some of the other database objects (listed as follows):

- **Stored procedures** are objects in the database for storing methods of actions. A procedure could be described as a program that processes actions in the database. For example, inserts, updates, and/or delete rows in a table.
- **Functions** are objects in the database that encapsulate formulas and calculations and return either scalar values, or sets of data.
- **Views** are an object that consists of one select-statement, and are referenced as a table. Normalized database views bring normalized data together and masks complex table structures.
- **Schemas** are an organizational object and can be described as a folder in a filesystem. All objects in a database must belong to a schema.
- **User-defined objects** are objects that consist of an interpretation of a native SQL Server data type and offer a standardized method of describing the value of columns, variables, and parameters.

SQL Server data types

The SQL Server Database Engine utilizes a wide selection of data types. A data type is a definition of how a value is structured, stored, and handled. There are data types for any kind of structured, semi-structured, and non-structured type of data.

Structured data types are native SQL Server data types such as `int`, `char`, `varchar`, `datetime`, `binary`, `varbinary`, `money`, `decimal`, `geography`, `geometry`, `location`, and so on. Character-based data types support both non-unicode, `char/varchar`, and unicode, `nchar/nvarchar`.

Semi-structured data types, such as `xml`, store their data in a structured manner internally and is usually handled by the database engine as large objects, but at the same time offers flexibility to add custom functions and indexes to efficiently display its content.

Non-structured data types are usually referred to as large objects called **blob (binary large objects)** or **clob (character large objects)** and used to store large amounts of data such as documents and binaries in the database. Also, `varbinary(max)`, `varchar(max)`, and `nvarchar (max)` are seen as non-structured objects. From the 2016 version , SQL Server had used a more modern approach and adequate data types for dealing with non-structured data: polybase feature and support for JSON.

Every data type offers specific features for a specific use. When designing a database, it's important to choose the right data type for every column of a table.

SQL/T-SQL basics

In this part of the chapter, you will get an introduction about SQL language, or to be more precise, the Microsoft version T-SQL (Transact-SQL). Before we actually start to write code, we will cover some basics about language SQL and T-SQL syntax. This knowledge is applicable in all the chapters that will come later, especially in Chapter 4, *Database in the Sandbox*, and Chapter 5, *Sample Databases*.

History of SQL/TSQL

During the seventies, the IBM research centre in San Jose, California created a research team named *System R* based on Edgar F. Codd's article *A Relational Model of Data for Large Shared Data Banks*. This later evolved into IBM System/38 in August of 1978. In 1986, the language **SQL (Structured Query Language)**, became an ANSI standard and in 1987 it was accepted as an ISO standard. Today, almost 40 years later, SQL is de facto standard when we are talking about retrieving and data processing.

In order to successfully write queries against SQL Server databases, you need to understand the query language **T-SQL (Transact-Structured Query Language)**. T-SQL, and both the ANSI and ISO standard, offers words such as SELECT, INSERT, UPDATE, and DELETE as well as FROM, JOIN, WHERE, GROUP BY, and ORDER BY to understand the syntax and what these words add to build better results when querying the database.

Even if the standards have minimal support for flow control, T-SQL offers additional scripting and batch processing flow control support such as IF...ELSE, WHILE.

Types of SQL statements

SQL/T-SQL consists of three main groups of statements:

DDL - Data Definition Language

- CREATE, to create database objects
- ALTER, to modify database objects
- DROP, to remove database objects

DCL - Data Control Language

- GRANT, to grant users permission to objects
- DENY, to deny users permissions to objects
- REVOKE, to remove either grant or deny

DML - Data Manipulation Language

- SELECT, to return rows of data from tables
- INSERT, to add rows of data to tables
- UPDATE, to modify rows of data in tables
- DELETE, to remove rows of data from tables

The next three chapters are focused on DDL, DML statements, and data retrieving techniques, from the SQL Server from a Linux point of view.

Working environments and tools

In Chapter 2, *Installation and Configuration*, we covered the installation procedure of SQL Server database engine and command-line tools. In this phase of development (CTP 1.3 - RC1) there is a limited number of tools to interact with SQL Server. But that will be changed in the near future. If this book was about the Windows platform, then content would likely be different, but this does not mean that we don't have quality tools to work with this database engine.

Here is a list of the most used currently supported tools on Linux and Windows platforms:

- sqlcmd (Linux)
- bpc (Linux)
- Visual Studio Code (Linux)
- SSMS (Windows)

sqlcmd

The command-line utility, sqlcmd, offers batch execution of T-SQL scripts and a simple utility for executing T-SQL statements. It will be our primary interaction interface with SQL Server database engine. If you want to connect to your SQL Server instance you will need to type sqlcmd and the following parameters: (-S server name, -U user name -P password) in your bash command line.

 You should avoid typing the password with parameter -P, because it will be visible on the screen. You can simply prevent this kind of situation in a matter skipping -P, and the database engine will ask your credentials after you press ENTER.

To connect on SQL Server, type the following command:

```
# sqlcmd -S sqlserver -U sa
```

In my case, the hostname is `sqlserver`; instead, you can type your IP address or `localhost`. After you press *Enter*, `sqlcmd` will ask you to provide a valid password for the sa account:

```
# Password:
```

If login credentials are OK, you will get a screen output as follows:

Figure 3-3. Successful login on SQL Server instance

Now, let's type your first SQL statement to check version number of your SQL Server database engine. As you can see in *Figure 3-3*, `sqlcmd` is numbering code lines, starting from 1. So, each time you press *Enter*, you will jump to the next line 2, 3, and so on. But when you need to execute your command (*Enter* is not enough), you will need to finish your statement with batch directive `GO`. Take a look at the following listing:

```
1> SELECT @@VERSION
2> GO
------------------------------------------------------------
Microsoft SQL Server vNext (CTP1.3) - 14.0.304.138 (X64)
        Feb 13 2017 16:49:12
        Copyright (C) 2016 Microsoft Corporation. All rights reserved.
        on Linux (openSUSE Leap 42.2

(1 rows affected)
```

First, we typed SELECT @@VERSION. After you press *Enter*, in the next line you need to type batch directive GO. Output (or result of execution) is an information message about SQL Server database engine and operating system version. Congratulations, you just finished your first SQL statement on a freshly installed SQL Server on Linux. It was not so hard. To exit in the bash command line, just type EXIT and press *Enter*. We will come back to sqlcmd in Chapter 4, *Database in the Sandbox*.

bcp

The bulk copy program bcp copies data between the same or different SQL Server instances. It can be used for import and export procedures. It is mostly used to import large numbers of rows into SQL Server databases or to export rows into data files. This utility requires no knowledge of SQL. One of the common usage scenarios is the **ETL** (**Extract Transform and Load**), process.

For example, to copy the content of a database table into a data file, you should write something like this (depends on your database and object names):

```
# bcp Northwind.Customers out "List of Customers.dat" -T -c
```

This command bulk copies the content of the Customers table from the Northwind database into a new file List of Customers.dat.

We will deal with bcp in the following chapters.

Visual Studio code

Now, something completely new. It is GUI code editor for Linux, macOS, and Windows. I don't know if you would believe me, but the vendor is also Microsoft. This is part of their new strategy to provide the power of Microsoft development tools on every major platform, not only Windows.

Visual Studio supports extensions for different kinds of development technologies and languages:

- C/C++
- Python
- SQL
- C#
- JavaScript

- PHP
- R
- XML
- And many more

From our point of view, Visual Studio code can directly communicate with SQL Server. Yes, this is a primary development tool, but it can be used to interact with database engines through SQL.

You can see how it looks in the following screenshot:

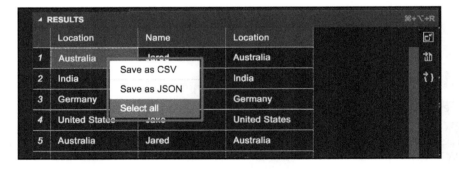

Figure 3-4. Writing SQL code trough Visual Studio Code editor

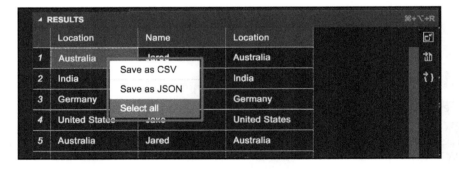

Figure 3-5. Browsing data and options for exporting

This tool is primarily for developers who use different kinds of programming languages. In the process, they can interact with SQL Server (on Linux and Windows) or many other database platforms. You can find more information on the tool here: `https://code.visual studio.com/`.

SQL Server Management Studio (SSMS)

SQL Server Management Studio (SSMS
(`https://docs.microsoft.com/en-us/sql/ssms/download-sql-server-management-studio-ssms`)), is the primary tool for both database administrators as well as database designers. It offers a graphical interface to write queries, server administration, and create database objects. Almost every action that can be carried out via dialog boxes and windows can also be done using SQL scripts. T-SQL also offers an advanced T-SQL editor with support for IntelliSense and code snippets together with full blown templates and linking into the Books Online.

Unfortunately, this tool is not supported on Linux platforms. This will probably change in the future. But don't look at this is as a limitation. If you have Windows installed (physical or virtual) you can install this free tool and connect to your (physical or virtual) Linux. This will require simultaneous usage of different platforms, but in today's IT world I believe that every IT professional uses more than one different operating system environment. The installation procedure is pretty simple and it requires no interaction.

 Before SQL Server 2016, SSMS was part of standard SQL Server installation. Now it is available as a separate download because faster development cycles.

The following steps describe how to connect to SQL Server on Linux with SQL Server Management Studio. To successfully do this, you will need the following:

- A Windows operating system with SSMS (physical or virtual)
- Linux with SQL Server on Linux (physical or virtual)
- The IP address of your SQL Server on Linux
- Login credentials
- Open TCP/IP port 1433 on Linux (default communication SQL Server port)

1. In the **Start** menu, locate **SQL Server Management Studio** and click on it. After SSMS starts, you should see something similar to the following:

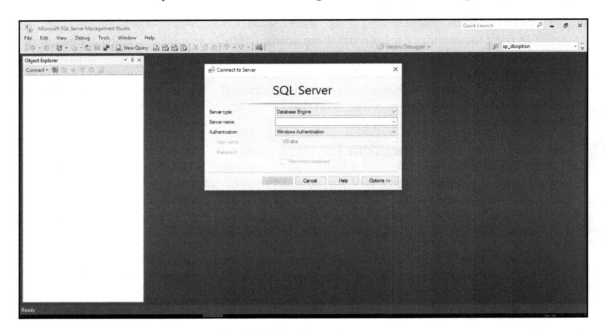

Figure 3-6. SSMS is awaiting connection parameters

The environment is not ready yet. Focus your attention on `Connect to Server` dialog windows, which expect some additional parameters:

- Service type
- Server name
- Authentication
- Username
- Password

2. For the **Server type**, we will choose **Database Engine**. In the field **Server name**, type the IP address of your Linux machine with SQL Server. Currently, SQL Server on Linux only supports SQL Server authentication. If you remember, during installation, you typed password for an sa user. Based on my configuration, **Connect to Server** dialog screen should look similar to the following screenshot:

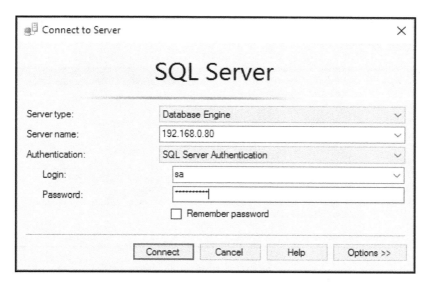

Figure 3-7. Connect to Server dialog windows with connection details

3. Click `Connect`. If your parameters are OK, then SSMS will initialize an environment to start interacting with the database engine.

4. From this point it is really easy to start. Every SQL query entered through SSMS or `sqlcmd` has the same results. The only difference is the luxury of GUI and the *military* style of Command Prompt. Let's try:

5. Press *Ctrl + N* to open new query windows.

6. Type the same command as in the `sqlcmd` case, `SELECT @@VERSION`.

While you are typing, IntelliSense will pop up with suggestions:

Figure 3-8. IntelliSense in action

7. Now press *F5*. Output will be similar to what is shown in the following screenshot:

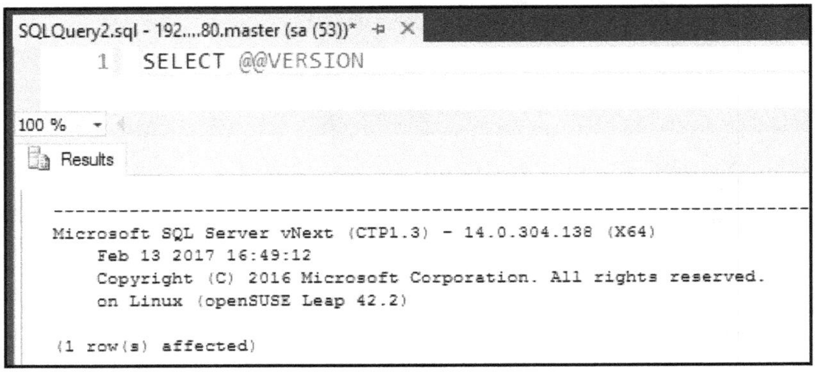

Figure 3-9. Result of query execution in GUI environment

It is much easier than in `sqlcmd`, but this not a native Linux environment and we will leave it for now. As I mentioned earlier, our focus is on command line.

Summary

In this chapter, we covered basics about SQL Server architecture and the major differences compared with classic SQL Server on Windows. Also, we explained basic tool usage that we will use in following chapters.

Now, prepare yourself for some real SQL coding in the next chapter.

4
Database in the Sandbox

The first major stop during our journey on SQL Server on Linux is SQL coding. To be more precise, we will write some DDL and DML statements which will provide us with a testing playground. That environment will be used now for practice and later when we need to use it again. This chapter is for all Linux users, and no SQL experience is necessary.

We will cover the following topics:

- DDL statements
- Creating a new database
- Creating new tables
- DML statements
- Data manipulation
- Creating database objects

DDL statements

DDL or **Data Definition Language** statements are a set of three simple but powerful and effective commands: CREATE, ALTER, and DROP. When you look at those words they do not provide you with enough information about what they are capable of doing. In a nutshell, you can do the following:

- CREATE: This statement will create anything from the server, down to the database level of objects (database, tables, views, stored procedures, triggers, users, encryption keys, and so on)
- ALTER: This gives you the option to modify any kind of object including server configuration and the database itself

- DROP: This is a dangerous but effective statement for deleting (dropping is the database term) server and database level of objects

As an example, the basic syntax for creating a new table looks like this:

```
CREATE TABLE [table name]
( [column definitions] ) [list of parameters]
```

Creating a new database

Before we create some tables and other database objects we need to set up our playground. I am assuming that you have some basic knowledge about databases, tables, data types, and relational modelling. However, don't you worry I'll lead you all the way:

1. First, connect to your SQL Server through the `sqlcmd` command-line tool:

   ```
   # sqlcmd -S sqlserver -U sa
   ```

2. Now, we will check how many databases we have on our instance by calling the `sys.databases` catalog view with the following statement:

   ```
   1> SELECT name FROM sys.databases
   2> GO
   name
   ----------------------------------
   master
   tempdb
   model
   msdb

   (4 rows affected)
   ```

3. As you can see, for now only the system databases are visible, but that is about to change.

4. Enter this CREATE statement in your `sqlcmd` to create a new database called University:

   ```
   1> CREATE DATABASE University
   2> GO
   ```

5. This tool does not tell you whether the database has been created, so you will need to repeat *step 2*. You should now see a new database on the list:

```
1> SELECT name FROM sys.databases
2> GO
name
-----------------------------------
master
tempdb
model
msdb
University

(5 rows affected)
```

6. Now, call the catalog view `sys.database_files` (https://msdn.microsoft.co m/en-us/library/ms174397.aspx), to see some detailed information about your new database. Be careful, this view has a large number of attributes and it will not be practical to see them all in the console. In my example, I will show just a small number of them:

```
1> USE University
2> GO
Changed database context to 'University'.
1> SELECT name, physical_name
2> FROM sys.database_files
3> GO
name physical_name
-----------------------------------------------------------
University C:\var\opt\mssql\data\University.mdf
University_log C:\var\opt\mssql\data\University_log.ldf

(2 rows affected)
```

Creating new tables

Now, we will create some basic table structures for our `University` database. Nothing too complicated, but you will get enough information about how SQL Server on Linux handles these requests. The idea is to practice a combination of DDL and DML statements in one project, from the database schema creation, to filling the database with some data, to changing the database structure, and finally by creating database objects to access the data.

The best way to explain this in practice is to create the following tables inside our University database:

- Students (basic personal data about students)
- Educators (basic personal data about teaching staff)
- Courses (tables to store information about courses)
- Grades (the central point of our system data about student's evaluation grades)

Our hypothetical system should look like the following figure:

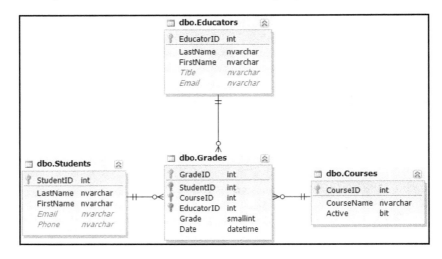

Figure 4-1. Database diagram for the University database

This schema does not describe a real-life university system, but the basic concepts, such as column definitions, data types, and primary and foreign keys, are the same whether there are 4 tables or 100 tables. All the concepts are contained within these simple four tables (entities), and are the foundation of every university information system. Let's start:

1. First, if you are not connected already, connect to your SQL server using the sqlcmd command-line tool.

2. Tell the SQL server that you want to work with the University database with the USE keyword:

```
1> USE University
2> GO
Changed database context to 'University'.
```

3. The next step is to create a `Students` table with the following columns: `StudentID`, `LastName` (15), `FirstName` (10), `Email` (15), and `Phone` (15):

```
1> CREATE TABLE Students (
2> StudentID int IDENTITY (1,1) PRIMARY KEY,
3> LastName nvarchar (15) NOT NULL,
4> FirstName nvarchar (10) NOT NULL,
5> Email nvarchar (15) NULL,
6> Phone nvarchar (15) NULL);
7> GO
```

4. Now let's define a table for the education staff: `EducatorID`, `LastName` (15), `FirstName` (10), `Title` (5), and `Email` (15):

```
1> CREATE TABLE Educators (
2> EducatorID int IDENTITY (1, 1) PRIMARY KEY,
3> LastName nvarchar (15) NOT NULL,
4> FirstName nvarchar (10) NOT NULL,
5> Title nvarchar (5) NULL,
6> Email nvarchar (15) NULL);
7> GO
```

5. The table for the courses should have the following definition: `CourseID`, `CourseName` (15), and `Active` (Boolean):

```
1> CREATE TABLE Courses (
2> CourseID int IDENTITY (1, 1) PRIMARY KEY,
3> CourseName nvarchar (15) NOT NULL,
4> Active bit NOT NULL);
5> GO
```

6. The last table will store students' grades and reference to other tables: `GradeID`, `StudentID`, `CourseID`, `EducatorID`, `Grade` (integer), and `Date` (date and time):

```
1> CREATE TABLE Grades (
2> GradeID int IDENTITY (1,1) PRIMARY KEY,
3> StudentID int NOT NULL CONSTRAINT FK_Students FOREIGN KEY
REFERENCES Students (StudentID),
4> CourseID int NOT NULL CONSTRAINT FK_Courses FOREIGN KEY
REFERENCES Courses (CourseID),
5> EducatorID int NOT NULL CONSTRAINT FK_Educators FOREIGN KEY
REFERENCES Educators (EducatorID),
6> Grade smallint NOT NULL,
7> Date datetime NOT NULL);
8> GO
```

7. Now, call the catalog view to see the list of newly created tables in the `University` database:

```
1> SELECT name,type_desc
2> FROM sys.objects
3> WHERE type = 'U'
4> GO
name type_desc
-----------------------------
Students USER_TABLE
Educators USER_TABLE
Courses USER_TABLE
Grades USER_TABLE
(4 rows affected)
```

DML statements

DML or **Data Manipulation Language** statements are a set of classic SQL commands used to work on the data (records inside the tables). They are: `INSERT`, `UPDATE`, `DELETE` and `SELECT`. We can use them directly (ad hoc) or through different sets of applications, as a CRUD layer (`CREATE`, `READ`, `UPDATE`, and `DELETE`). Here are the explanations of DML commands:

- `INSERT`: Adding new records in to tables
- `UPDATE`: Modifying existing rows inside the tables
- `DELETE`: Removing records from the tables
- `SELECT`: Read-only access to the records stored inside the tables

We will learn more about `SELECT` in `Chapter 6`, *A Crash Course in Querying*.

Data manipulation

Now, we will start working with concrete data based on the foundation that we've created in the previous steps. So, we will use our `University` database to enter initial data into tables and test basic manipulation with the data:

1. If you are not already in it, change the focus of the current database to `University`:

```
1> USE University
2> GO
Changed database context to 'University'.
```

2. First, let's add one student into the `Students` table with a single `INSERT` statement:

```
1> INSERT INTO Students
2> VALUES ('Azemović','Imran','Imran@dba.ba', NULL)
3> GO
(1 rows affected)
```

3. In this step, we will add two new students with a single `INSERT` statement, another cool SQL Server feature:

```
1> INSERT INTO Students
2> VALUES ('Avdić','Selver', NULL, NULL),
3> ('Azemović','Sara','Sara@dba','000-111-222'),
4> ('Mušić','Denis','Denis@dba.ba, NULL)
5> GO
(3 rows affected)
```

4. Now, let's check the content of the `Student` table:

```
1> SELECT * FROM Students
2> GO
StudentID    LastName          FirstName    Email              Phone
-----------  ----------------  -----------  ----------------   -----------
          1  Azemovic          Imran        Imran@dba.ba       NULL
          2  Avdic             Selver       NULL               NULL
          3  Azemovic          Sara         Sara@dba           000-111-222
          4  Music             Denis        Denis@dba.ba       NULL

(4 rows affected)
```

5. One student is sent a request to add an email address. The following `UPDATE` command will do the job:

```
1> UPDATE Students
2> SET Email = 'Selver@dba.ba'
3> WHERE StudentID = 2
4> GO
(1 rows affected)
```

6. It is time to delete one record, because `Denis` should not be on the student list since he is one of the teaching staff:

```
1> DELETE FROM Students
2> WHERE StudentID = 4
3> GO
(1 rows affected)
```

7. Again, let's check the contents of the `Students` table:

```
1> SELECT * FROM Students
2> GO
StudentID    LastName              FirstName    Email               Phone
-----------  --------------------  -----------  ------------------  -----------
          1  Azemovic              Imran        Imran@dba.ba        NULL
          2  Avdic                 Selver       NULL                NULL
          3  Azemovic              Sara         Sara@dba            000-111-222
(3 rows affected)
```

8. Using the same principle, we will add a couple of records to the `Educators` table:

```
1> INSERT INTO Educators
2> VALUES ('Vejzovic','Zanin','Ph.D.',NULL),
3> ('Music','Denis','Ph.D.',NULL),
4> ('Bevanda','Vanja','Ph.D.','Vanja@dba.ba')
5> GO
(3 rows affected)
```

9. Now, we will add some courses:

```
1> INSERT INTO Courses
2> VALUES ('Programming',1),
3> ('Databases',1),
4> ('Networks',1)
5> GO
(3 rows affected)
```

10. The final step is to enter one grade and to check the content of the `Grades` table:

```
1> INSERT INTO Grades
2> VALUES (1,2,3,10,GETDATE())
3> GO
(1 rows affected)

1> SELECT * FROM Grades
2> GO
```

```
GradeID      StudentID    CourseID     EducatorID   Grade   Date
-----------  -----------  -----------  -----------  ------  -----------
          1            1            2            3      10  2017-03-23
(1 rows affected)
```

This DML practice will be enough to understand the basic concepts of adding, modifying, and deleting data. If you don't have any SQL experience it is a good start from which to continue exploring on your own. If you have experience with another data platform, such as MySQL, PostgreSQL, and so on, then you will see differences in using SQL Server on Linux.

Changing table definition

Sometimes you simply can't implement all the tables' attributes. One of the reasons is that in the moment you may not know all the business requirements and will not be able to define a stable table structure. The SQL language gives you the power to do that even if tables have records inside.

Let's add a new `PhoneNumber` column to the `Educators` table:

1. In this scenario, we will use the `ALTER TABLE` statement:

   ```
   1> ALTER TABLE Educators
   2> ADD PhoneNumber nvarchar (15) NULL
   3> GO
   ```

2. Now, we will alter the `Students` table to add the new column, set default values, and place a unique constraint on it. A unique constraint is used when we need to ensure some values are unique in the table but without using primary keys:

   ```
   1> ALTER TABLE Students
   2> ADD UserName nvarchar (15) NOT NULL DEFAULT 'user.name'
   3> WITH VALUES
   4> GO
   1> UPDATE Students
   2> SET UserName = Email
   3> GO
   1> CREATE UNIQUE NONCLUSTERED INDEX UQ_user_name
   2> ON dbo.Students (UserName)
   3> GO
   ```

3. Okay, let's add a new record to test the column constraint:

```
1> INSERT INTO Students
2> (FirstName, LastName, UserName)
3> VALUES
4> ('John','Doe','john.doe')
5> GO
```

4. For some reason, the student with `ID = 1` wants to add a user name, but it is already been taken by a different user. The database engine will throw an error and state that this operation is not valid:

```
1> UPDTAE Students
2> SET UserName = 'john.doe'
3> WHERE StudentID = 1
4> GO
Msg 2627, Level 14, State 1, Server openSUSE, Line 1
Violation of UNIQUE KEY constraint 'UQ_user_name'. Cannot insert
duplicate key in object 'dbo.Students'. The duplicate key value is
(john.doe).
The statement has been terminated.
```

Dropping a table

Finally, the last table operation to look at is dropping. To use Windows terminology, you can think of it like a delete but without the Recycle Bin. It will delete all the records and table definitions:

1. First, we will create a simple table:

```
1> CREATE TABLE Test
2> (Column1 int, Column2 int)
3> GO
```

2. The next step is to make it vanish from our database:

```
1> DROP TABLE Test
2> GO
```

 In the same way, you can delete any object from a database:
`DROP object type (object name)`

Creating other database objects

After tables and playing with DML statements, we are ready to look at another set of database objects. These are also important from the perspective of data access and are heavily used by developers during the application development process. Of course, they can be used for direct data access and modification without an application layer. We will cover the following objects:

- Views
- Stored procedures
- Triggers

Again, as in previous examples, we will not go into much technical detail. But it will give you enough information to explore this topic further on your own.

Creating views

Views are objects that consist of the SELECT statement, and are referenced as a table. Normalized database views bring normalized data together and mask the complexity of the table structures.

Another use of views is a security purpose. Let's say that, of 10 columns inside your table, two of them are not for public viewing. Creating a view to access the rest of the public columns is the most effective and easiest way of implementation. However, be aware that a view is not essentially a security feature.

1. We want to create a view to show only FirtsName, LastName, and Email columns from the Students table and corresponding data. To do that, type the following statement:

```
1> CREATE VIEW vStudents
2> AS
3> SELECT FirstName, LastName, Email
4> FROM Students
5> GO
```

2. The next step is to check it is working as expected. Type the following SELECT statement on the view, not the table:

```
1> SELECT * FROM vStudents
2> GO
FirstName    LastName         Email
----------   ----------------  ---------------
Azemovic     Imran            Imran@dba.ba
Avdic        Selver           NULL
Azemovic     Sara             Sara@dba.ba
John         Doe              NULL
(4 rows affected)
```

Working with views is the same as with tables. After the next two chapters, you will be able to combine and create more sophisticated views and queries on your SQL Server on Linux.

Creating stored procedures

Stored procedures are objects in the database for storing methods of action. A procedure could be described as a program that processes actions in the database. For example, inserts, updates, and/or deletes rows in a table:

1. In the following demonstration, you will create a stored procedure for searching. It will take StudentID as the dynamic parameter and show the result based on that. In the sqlcmd, type following SQL code:

```
1> CREATE PROCEDURE usp_Student_search_byID
2> @StudentID int
3> AS
4> SELECT StudentID, LastName, FirstName, Email
5> FROM Students
6> WHERE StudentID = @StudentID
7> GO
```

2. If you want to execute a stored procedure, you can do it two ways: ad hoc, through the database administration and development tools (sqlcmd, SSMS, and so on); or you can call it directly from the application layer (web or mobile) and provide the input parameters. In our case, it will use an ad hoc approach:

```
1> EXEC usp_Student_search_byID 1
2> GO
StudentID    LastName        FirstName  Email
-----------  --------------  ---------- ------------
          1  Azemovic        Imran      Imran@dba.ba

(1 rows affected)
```

3. As you can see, we had provided an input parameter to @StudentID, in this case StudentID is 1.

Creating triggers

Triggers are event-based SQL code. They are commonly used when we need to execute some specific operation (SQL code) after, before, or instead of some user action. For example, when a user deletes a record from the database, a trigger can store the original data. The scope of its usage is really wide.

You will create a trigger that will prevent any dropping of database objects (accidental or not). Now type the following trigger definition:

```
1> CREATE TRIGGER Dropping_prevention
2> ON DATABASE
3> FOR DROP_TABLE, DROP_VIEW, DROP_PROCEDURE
4> AS
5> PRINT 'Deleting is not permitted, this operation is logged!'
6> ROLLBACK
7> GO
```

Now is the moment of truth. We will try to drop a stored procedure that we created in the previous steps:

```
1> DROP PROCEDURE usp_Student_search_byID
2> GO
Deleting is not permitted, this operation is logged!
Msg 3609, Level 16, State 2, Server openSUSE, Line 1
The transaction ended in the trigger. The batch has been aborted.
```

Summary

In this chapter, you have learned how to create a learning or test environment on your SQL Server on Linux. You now know how to create a database, tables, and other database objects, such as views, stored procedures, and triggers. Also, you are familiar with how to deal with data. After the next two chapters, you will be able to combine all your knowledge to create some really impressive work.

In the next chapter, you will learn how to deal with SQL Server sample databases, where to find them, and how to install them. Those environments are ideal to learn administration tasks and train your SQL language skills from this chapter.

5
Sample Databases

In the previous chapter, you learned how to create a learning environment and started writing some serious SQL code. However, our database lacks data and complexity, which we need in order to practice and test all the cool SQL language features on SQL Server on Linux. This chapter will guide you through some of the best sample databases which can be used to test almost any SQL Server feature and prepare yourself for the production environment. Before beginning with the samples, I will briefly explain the basics about relational database concepts and the process of normalization.

We will cover the following topics:

- Relational database concepts
- Normalization
- `Northwind` database
- Pubs database
- `AdventureWorks` database
- `WideWorldImporters` database

Relational database concepts

Relational databases consist of many objects, and the most common of these is a table. A table is a logical structure (relation) for storing and retrieving rows of data. It is defined by its columns which are represented by the data types.

Every table should have a primary key as a unique representation of a single row. It is usually a single column that either hosts a sequential number or a unique identifier that would never be used more than once. Tables can also contain two or more columns that together represent the unique row of the table. A table can also host foreign keys which describe its table reference, or relation to another table. For example, a `Students` table has a unique `StudentID` column, and the same `StudentID` is then represented in a `Grades` table to tie the actual grade to the student. This allows for one student to have none, one, or many grades, and requires that student record to exist before the grades can be entered.

Normalization

Modelling, or designing, a database is deciding which tables and columns, together with other objects, are needed to support the application that consumes the data. As applications work with objects and attributes, a common mistake is to create a physical table structure as a copy of the object model. Even if the database supports the object model, the main responsibility of the database is to handle data. When different objects share the same types of data, the database designer needs to look further and model the table based on the types of data.

Database normalization is the process that seeks to eliminate the need for multiple repetitions of the same data. It implies a specific form of field and table organization that will minimize data redundancy and dependency. Therefore, the process of normalization often requires the division of large tables into smaller (and less redundant) tables and defined relationships between them. The objective is to isolate data so that additions, deletions, and modifications of a field can be made in just one table and then propagated through the rest of the database via the defined relationships.

In June 1970, Edgar F Codd published an article, *A Relational Model of Data for Large Shared Data Banks*, in which he introduced the concept of normalization and what we now know as the **first normal form** (**1NF**) that laid the groundwork for the theory of relational databases and the rules for how they should be constructed. *Codd's 12 rules* are a set of thirteen rules numbered 0 to 12 that describe the requirements for what should be considered as a relational database.

Codd went on to also define the **second normal form** (**2NF**) and **third normal form** (**3NF**).

First normal form

Every table must uniquely represent each row, not carry any duplicate rows, and not have any repeating groups. For example, a `Students` table, with the attributes:

- `Name`
- `City`
- `EmailAddress`
- `PhoneNumber1`
- `PhoneNumber2`

The `PhoneNumber` attributes are a repeating group and the table should consist of four columns:

- `Name`
- `City`
- `EmailAddress`
- `PhoneNumber`

Second normal form

The table must meet the criteria of 1NF and any of the non-key attributes cannot rely on a subset of the key. As a student might have several phone numbers, this model might generate many rows for one person (redundancy). If hypothetically speaking, `Name` uniquely represents a student, the model should be: `Students` (`Name`, `City`, `EmailAddress`) and `PhoneNumbers` (`Name`, `PhoneNumber`).

Third normal form

The table must meet the criteria of 2NF and every non-key attribute is directly dependent on its key, a super key. For example, a students table: Students (StudentKey, Name, Department, DepartmentLocation). DepartmentLocation is dependent on the department, not the employee. To adhere to the 3NF a better solution would be Locations (LocationKey, Name), Departments (DepartmentKey, Name, LocationKey), and Employees (EmployeeKey, Name, DepartmentKey).

Northwind database

If you are familiar with the classic SQL Server on Windows then there is only a very small probability that you haven't heard about the epic Northwind. Actually, this database originated from the ancient Microsoft Access. Those members of the Linux population with some MySQL or PostgreSQL experience probably do not know about it, but it is very close to the sakila or dvdrental samples from those platforms.

Northwind (https://northwinddatabase.codeplex.com/) is a classic example of a sales system where you have basic entities: Customers, Products, Orders, and Employees. From the SQL Server perspective, it was an official example from version SQL Server 2000 to SQL Server 2005. Later it was replaced by a more detailed and complex system of sales. Now, Northwind is not officially supported by Microsoft, but it remains one of the most popular examples in the SQL Server world as it is simple, easy to read, and ideal for beginners with zero or very little database and SQL experience.

As you can see in *Figure 5-1*, Northwind has 13 tables with a very clear set of names of the tables and table attributes. From the data perspective, the content is small but very clear and easy to understand:

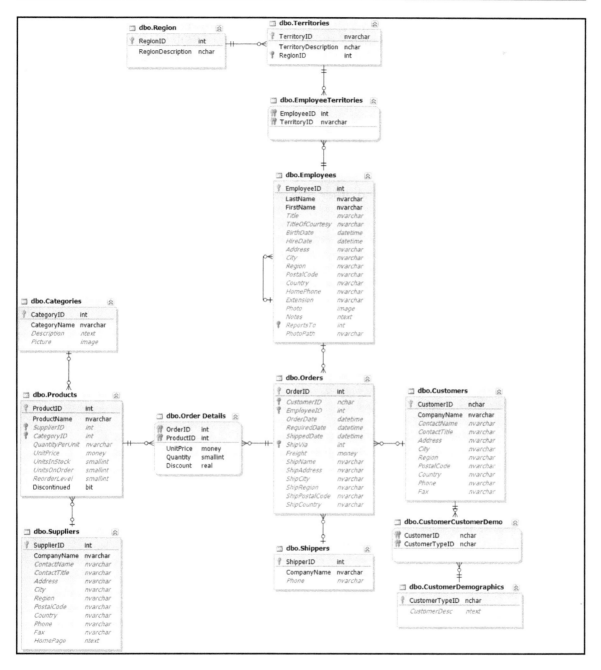

Figure 5-1. Northwind database relational schema

You can test and practice almost any SQL Server on Linux feature with the Northwind database. You can download and install this database on your SQL Server instance from `http://www.microsoft.com/en-us/download/details.aspx?id=23654`.

Pubs database

The hall of fame would not be complete if I did not mention the `Pubs` (`http://www.microsoft.com/en-us/download/details.aspx?id=23654`) sample database. If sales are not good enough for you, then publishing is the right choice. Here you can find `authors`, `titles`, `publishers`, and other entities regarding a publishing business:

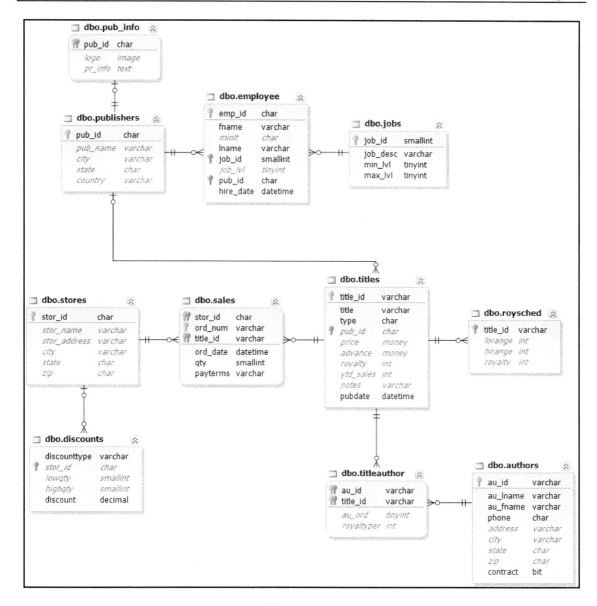

Figure 5-2. Pubs database relational schema

Objects and table attribute names are a less clear, because the author of this database sample has preferred the use of short words, `qty`, `au_lname`, `highqty`, and so on. However, with 11 tables it is quite simple and easy to understand.

You can download this sample at
`http://www.microsoft.com/en-us/download/details.aspx?id=23654`. Pubs originated
from Accent SQL Server 2000, but it can be used for practicing SQL and DBA tasks.

In `Chapter 7`, *Backup Operations*, we will learn how to restore those databases. If you are
eager you can jump quickly to `Chapter 8`, *User Management*, and study how to do it.

AdventureWorks database

From SQL Server 2005 until 2016, this has been the new example. We can see it as like
`Northwind` on steroids. In the last official version, `AdventureWorks` database included 71
user tables, which is more than five times larger than `Northwind`. Don't panic, it is just a
good old customer-sales system but with more detail. `Northwind` deals with seafood, while
`AdventureWorks` is about selling bicycles.

One of the biggest complaints about the previous examples is that they are not complex
enough to present adequate real-life database system environments. If we just look at the
partial list of tables we will get a picture:

```
Name
------------------------------
Address
AddressType
AWBuildVersion
BillOfMaterials
BusinessEntity
BusinessEntityAddress
BusinessEntityContact
ContactType
CountryRegion
CountryRegionCurrency
CreditCard
Culture
Currency
CurrencyRate
Customer
DatabaseLog
Department
Document
EmailAddress
Employee
EmployeeDepartmentHistory
EmployeePayHistory
ErrorLog
```

```
Illustration
JobCandidate
Location
Password
Person
PersonCreditCard
PersonPhone
PhoneNumberType
Product
ProductCategory
ProductCostHistory
ProductDescription
ProductDocument
...
(71 row(s) affected)
```

The database diagram can't fit onto one page of this book. Even A4 would be tight, so let me just show you just one small part of the system. The following picture illustrates the HR division of the `AdventureWorks` hypothetical corporation:

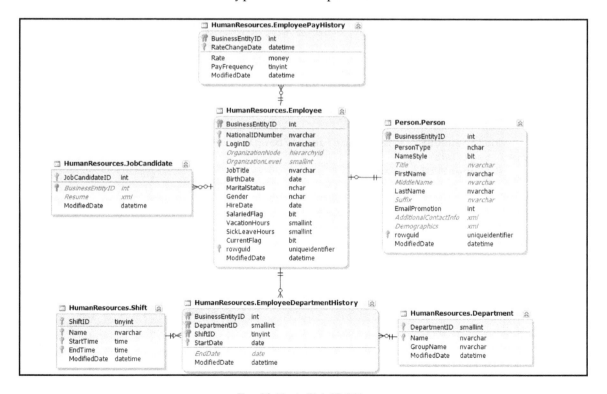

Figure 5-3. AdventureWorks HR division

This database goes way beyond the classic system for learning, but here you can test almost any type of query or admin task that can be close to a real-life scenario. In the next chapter, some of the examples we use will be on this database. Now, I will explain how to install this database on your SQL Server on Linux.

Installing AdventureWorks

The following steps will install `AdventureWorks` on SQL Server on Linux:

1. The first step is to download a backup file to your default location:
   - **From**: `http://msftdbprodsamples.codeplex.com/releases/view/125550`
   - **To**: `/home/Downloads/`
   - **Filename**: In my case that is: `Adventure Works 2014 Full Database Backup.zip`

2. Unzip the `AdventureWorks2014.bak` file

3. Now create a folder for all your backups with root privileges (`sudo su`) through bash:

   ```
   dba@openSUSE:~> sudo su
   dba@openSUSE:~> mkdir -p /var/opt/mssql/backup
   ```

4. Move `AdventureWorks2014.bak` into the `backup` folder:

   ```
   dba@openSUSE:~> mv /home/user1/Downloads/AdventureWorks2014.bak /var/opt/mssql/backup/
   dba@openSUSE:~> exit
   ```

5. Last but not least, restore the BAK file into the `AdventureWorks` sample database:

```
1> RESTORE DATABASE AdventureWorks
2> FROM DISK = '/var/opt/mssql/backup/AdventureWorks2014.bak'
3> WITH MOVE 'AdventureWorks2014_Data' TO
'/var/opt/mssql/data/AdventureWorks2014_Data.mdf',
      4> MOVE 'AdventureWorks2014_Log' TO
'/var/opt/mssql/data/AdventureWorks2014_Log.ldf'
      5> GO
```

6. Now try to change the working database to see if everything is okay:

```
1> USE AdventureWorks
2> GO
```

If the default database I changed, then the restore operation was successful. Don't you worry, if you don't fully understand `RESTORE DATABASE`. It will be clear in `Chapter 7`, *Backup Operations*. In this phase, it is important that you have working and testing environments.

WideWorldImporters database

This database (`https://github.com/Microsoft/sql-server-samples/releases/tag/wide-world-importers-v1.0`) is the latest one and fully compatible with all features in SQL Server 2016 and beyond, and it is the most complex. If you are planning to learn or develop your SQL skills, I highly recommend not starting with `WideWordlImporters` until you have sufficient knowledge about SQL Server specific features, such as temporal tables, in-memory OLTP, data masking, and so on.

This database contains a lot of useful gems, just waiting to be explored, and based on the examples, implemented inside your own projects. The following diagram, *Figure 5-4*, only illustrates one small part of the database:

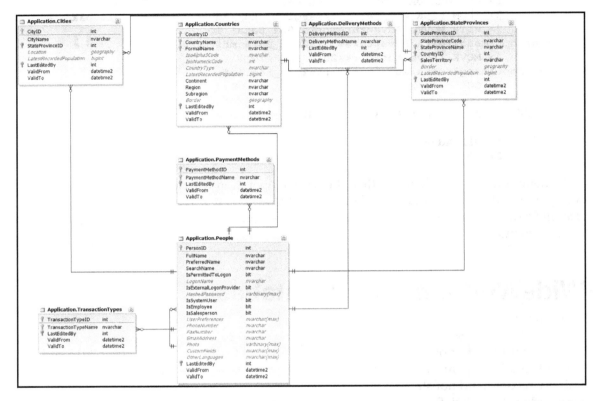

Figure 5-4. WideWordlImporters locations section

```
name
-------------------------------
BuyingGroups
BuyingGroups_Archive
Cities
Cities_Archive
ColdRoomTemperatures
ColdRoomTemperatures_Archive
Colors
Colors_Archive
Countries
Countries_Archive
CustomerCategories
CustomerCategories_Archive
```

```
Customers
Customers_Archive
CustomerTransactions
DeliveryMethods
DeliveryMethods_Archive
InvoiceLines
Invoices
OrderLines
Orders
PackageTypes
PackageTypes_Archive
PaymentMethods
PaymentMethods_Archive
People
People_Archive
PurchaseOrderLines
PurchaseOrders
SpecialDeals
StateProvinces
StateProvinces_Archive
StockGroups
StockGroups_Archive
StockItemHoldings
StockItems
StockItems_Archive
StockItemStockGroups
StockItemTransactions
SupplierCategories
SupplierCategories_Archive
Suppliers
Suppliers_Archive
SupplierTransactions
SystemParameters
TransactionTypes
TransactionTypes_Archive
VehicleTemperatures

(48 row(s) affected)
```

Summary

In this chapter, you learned what the SQL Server sample databases are. Also, you know what the process of normalization is and how to recognize normal forms based on the entity attributes. Finally, you learned how to install the `AdventureWorks` sample, which we will be using in the next chapter.

In the next chapter, you will learn new, or improve you current, SQL coding skills through a crash course of querying. The reason is very simple, if you are dealing with databases then you should speak SQL.

6
A Crash Course in Querying

Databases are one of the cornerstones of modern businesses. Data retrieval is usually made with a SELECT statement and it's therefore very important that you are familiar with this part of your journey. Retrieved data is often not organized in the way you want it to be, so it requires additional formatting. Besides formatting, accessing very large amounts of data requires you to take into account the speed and manner of query execution, which can have a major impact on system performance.

This chapter will be your guide through the basic elements of the SELECT statement, the last of the DML commands that we haven't yet covered in detail. To cover all the elements and scenarios we would need at least another book.

We will cover the following topics:

- Retrieving and filtering data
- Summarizing data
- Querying multiple tables

Retrieving and filtering data

As you will have noticed, databases usually consist of many tables where all the data is stored. The AdventureWorks database contains 71 tables, including tables for Customers, Products, Orders, and so on. The table names clearly describe the data that is stored in the table. If you need to create a list of new products, or a list of customers who ordered the most products, you would retrieve this information by creating a query. A query is an enquiry into the database made by using the SELECT statement. The SELECT statement is the first and most fundamental SQL statement that we are going to introduce in this chapter.

The SELECT statement consists of a set of clauses that specifies which data will be included into a query result set. All the clauses of SQL statements are the keywords and, because of that, are written in capital letters. A syntactically correct SELECT statement requires a mandatory FROM clause which specifies the source of the data you want to retrieve. Besides mandatory clauses, there are a few optional clauses that can be used to filter and organize data:

- INTO: Enables you to insert data (retrieved by the SELECT clause) into a different table, it is mostly used to create table backups
- WHERE: Places conditions on a query and eliminates rows that would be returned by a query without any conditions
- ORDER BY: Displays the query result in either ascending or descending alphabetical order
- GROUP BY: Provides a mechanism for arranging identical data into groups
- HAVING: Allows you to create selection criteria at the group level

Retrieving data from a table

The SELECT clause in a query is followed by a list of the comma separated column names that you wish to retrieve in a result set.

From this point onwards, I will assume that you know how to start sqlcmd and connect to your SQL Server on Linux instance and the sample database, AdventureWorks. For the sake of simplicity, where the result set provides a reasonable amount of data, I will use the TOP operator. TOP can limit the result set to an exact number of rows. For example, SELECT TOP 3 Name FROM Production.Product will return only the first three rows from this table.

The following code sample retrieves data from the ProductNumber and Name columns stored inside the Product table:

```
1> USE AdventureWorks
2> GO
Changed database context to 'AdventureWorks'.
1> SELECT TOP 5 ProductNumber, Name
2> FROM Production.Product
3> GO


ProductNumber                Name
------------------------     ------------------------
AR-5381                      Adjustable Race
BA-8327                      Bearing Ball
BE-2349                      BB Ball Bearing
BE-2908                      Headset Ball Bearings
BL-2036                      Blade

(5 rows affected)
```

As a result of the query execution, we received only five records from the entire table (504 rows in total) that include only data on product name and number. In order to retrieve all the columns from the Production.Product table you can use a wildcard character (*) that means *all columns*:

```
1> SELECT *
2> FROM Production.Product
3> GO
```

However, especially when working with a production database, SELECT * should be avoided unless you really need to retrieve all columns. Depending on the amount of retrieved data, use of the wildcard character can cause not only server and network performance reduction, but also a result set that is difficult to read and analyze.

String functions

String data manipulation is mostly used in cases when it is necessary to represent strings in a format that is different from the one stored in the table; for example, to extract substrings, change letter case, and so on. The easiest way to manipulate string data is to use string functions that take a character string as input and produce another character string as output. Some of the most commonly used string functions are: SUBSTRING, LEFT, RIGHT, UPPER, LOWER, LEN, and DATALENGTH.

Let us take a look at each one in detail:

- SUBSTRING: Returns part of an expression passed in as an argument. The following example extracts a substring from the expression SQL Server loves Linux and which starts from the eighteenth character and is five characters long:

```
1> SELECT SUBSTRING ('SQL Server loves Linux', 18, 5)
2> GO
-----
Linux
(1 rows affected)
```

- LEFT, RIGHT: Returns the specified number of characters from one side (left or right) of the expression:

```
1> SELECT LEFT ('SQL Server loves Linux', 3)
2> GO
---
SQL
(1 rows affected)
```

- UPPER, LOWER: Returns uppercase or lowercase versions of all characters in the expression:

```
1> SELECT UPPER ('SQL Server loves Linux')
2> GO
--------------------
SQL SERVER LOVES LINUX
(1 rows affected)
```

- REPLACE: Replaces the occurrence of the string specified as the search string (Linux) with a replacement string (openSUSE):

```
1> SELECT REPLACE ('SQL Server loves Linux', 'Linux', 'openSUSE')
2> GO
------------------------
SQL Server loves openSUSE
(1 rows affected)
```

- LEN, DATALENGTH: The LEN function returns the length (number of characters) of a string expression, while DATALENGTH returns the number of bytes used to represent any expression:

```
1> SELECT LEN ('SQL Server loves Linux')
2> GO
----------------
              22
(1 rows affected)
```

Exercise

Your company manager requires a list of all products, which should contain a product number and color next to the product name. Product names should all be capitalized and the list should omit the product initials (the first two characters) but include the rest of the product number:

```
1> SELECT TOP 5 UPPER (Name),
2> SUBSTRING (ProductNumber, 4, 6), Color
3> FROM Production.Product
4> GO
```

		Color
ADJUSTABLE RACE	5381	NULL
BEARING BALL	8327	NULL
BB BALL BEARING	2349	NULL
HEADSET BALL BEARINGS	2908	NULL
BLADE	2036	NULL

```
(5 rows affected)
```

Filtering data

In practice, there are very few cases where you want to show all the data contained in the table. Therefore, most of the time you will need data that meets certain conditions or, in other words, you will need filtered data. By using the WHERE clause in the SELECT statement, you can specify search conditions and return only those rows (records) that meet specific criteria. The conditions that are specified in the WHERE clauses are known as predicates and, in most cases, they result in one of the Boolean values TRUE or FALSE. However, predicates can result in an UNKNOWN value which will be discussed later in the chapter. Let's look at an example that creates a list of products that can be manufactured in 2 days. The number of days necessary to manufacture products is stored as an integer value in column DaysToManufacture:

```
1> SELECT ProductNumber, Color
2> FROM Production.Product
3> WHERE DaysToManufacture = 2
4> GO
```

```
ProductNumber          Color
-------------------    ---------------
   FR-M94B-38              Black
   FR-M94S-38              Silver
   FR-M63B-38              Black
   FR-R72Y-38              Yellow
   FR-M63S-38              Silver
   FR-M21B-40              Black
   FR-M21S-40              Silver

(7 rows affected)
```

Comparison operators

Comparison operators are used when it is necessary to compare data from the table with a specific value or expression. It is important to note that you can compare only compatible values which are defined by a data type. This means that you will not be able to compare the string with decimal values. The following is a list of the basic comparison operators that can be used in the WHERE clause:

Operator	Description
=	equals
<>, !=	does not equal
>	is greater than
<	is less than
>=	is greater than or equal to
<=	is less than or equal to

The next example returns a list of products whose weight is greater than or equal to 1,000:

```
1> SELECT Name, Weight
2> FROM Production.Product
3> WHERE Weight >= 1000
4> GO

Name                               Weight
---------------------------------  ----------
LL Road Rear Wheel                 1050.00
ML Road Rear Wheel                 1000.00

(2 rows affected)
```

String comparison

In addition to the basic operators described, SQL also supports comparison operators for evaluating string data types. The most basic form of string comparison can be made with the equal (=) operator as shown in the next example which retrieves the Name and ProductNumber of the product named Chainring:

```
1> SELECT Name
2> FROM Production.Product
3> WHERE Name = 'Chainring'
4> GO

Name
--------------------------------
Chainring

(1 rows affected)
```

In order to create more complex comparisons, you will need to use some of the advanced mechanisms such as LIKE. This operator is used in cases when search criteria are only partially known. In order to specify the missing parts of the value, you can use one of the following wildcard characters:

Wildcard character	Description
% (percent)	Replaces zero or more characters
_ (underscore)	Replaces a single character
[]	Replaces any single character within the specified range or set of characters
[^]	Replaces any single character NOT in the specified range or set of characters

For example, if you are not sure what the exact product name is but you know it does not start with A and that its third character is f, then you can use the following query:

```
1> SELECT Name
2> FROM Production.Product
3> WHERE Name LIKE '[^A]_f%'
4> GO

Name
--------------------------------------------------
Reflector

(1 rows affected)
```

Logical operators

If the search criteria require more than one condition to be specified, then those conditions need to be connected with logical operators AND, OR, and NOT. Expression evaluation with logical operators usually results with a Boolean value TRUE or FALSE.

Let us go through each one in detail:

- AND: Results with TRUE only when the left and the right expressions are TRUE. The next query will return the top three rows from Products table where ListPrice is less than 2,000 and it takes no longer than one day to manufacture them.

```
1> SELECT TOP 3 ProductNumber, ListPrice, DaysToManufacture
2> FROM Production.Product
3> WHERE ListPrice < 2000 AND DaysToManufacture = 1
4> GO
ProductNumber      ListPrice      DaysToManufacture
----------------   ------------   ------------------
BE-2349            .0000          1
BL-2036            .0000          1
CS-2812            .0000          1
(3 rows affected)
```

- OR: Results with TRUE when either expression is TRUE. Therefore, the execution of the previous query with the OR logical operator will result with 469 rows (including all rows that can be manufactured in one day or with a ListPrice is less than 2,000):

```
1> SELECT TOP 3 ProductNumber, ListPrice, DaysToManufacture
2> FROM Production.Product
3> WHERE ListPrice < 2000 OR DaysToManufacture = 1
4> GO
```

- NOT: Results with the reversed value of any other Boolean operator. The following query will return all rows whose ListPrice is not less than 2,000, or in other words it will return all rows whose ListPrice is greater than or equal to 2,000:

```
1> SELECT TOP 3 ProductNumber, ListPrice, DaysToManufacture
2> FROM Production.Product
3> WHERE NOT ListPrice < 2000
4> GO
```

Working with NULL values

One of the issues that occurs regularly when working with databases is an absent, incomplete, or unavailable value. In order to overcome these issues, SQL uses so-called 3-valued logic where expressions can either have a value, have no value (NULL), or be UNKNOWN (caused by the existence of a NULL value in the expression). A NULL is an undefined value and it's usually used as a temporary value that will later be updated with some real data. In the context of numeric or string data, NULL is not the same as zeros or blanks since they are both defined values.

Considering that NULL is used to represent a missing value, there are several rules that should be borne in mind:

- Any arithmetic or comparison operation that involves a NULL value will result with NULL value:
  - 50 + NULL -> NULL
  - 50 < NULL -> NULL
- When one of the conditions in the WHERE clause results with NULL , it is treated as FALSE.
- It is important to note that NULL values can't be compared using standard comparison operators and therefore you will have to use the keyword IS NULL. The following query will return the top five rows whose color is NULL:

```
1> SELECT TOP 5 Name, Color
2> FROM Production.Product
3> WHERE Color IS NULL
4> GO
Name                                               Color
-------------------------------------------------- --------
Adjustable Race                                    NULL
Bearing Ball                                       NULL
BB Ball Bearing                                    NULL
Headset Ball Bearings                              NULL
Blade                                              NULL
 (5 rows affected)
```

The keyword IS NULL can also be used in combination with the negation NOT, so you can write this condition: WHERE Color IS NOT NULL.

However, sometimes you want to make NULL values part of the result set but in a form that is understandable to people. One way is to adjust the NULL value to the end user and replace it with other more appropriate terms such as N/A (not applicable). These adjustments can be made by using the IS NULL function:

```
1> SELECT TOP 5 Name, ISNULL (Color, 'N/A')
2> FROM Production.Product
3> GO
Name

---------------------------------------------------  -------
Adjustable Race                                       N/A
Bearing Ball                                          N/A
BB Ball Bearing                                       N/A
Headset Ball Bearings                                 N/A
Blade                                                 N/A
(5 rows affected)
```

Manipulating query output

By default, records in a result set are ordered in the same way they were entered into the table. If you want to modify the default order of records in a result set, you can use the ORDER BY clause. This clause enables you to specify ascending (keyword ASC) or descending (keyword DESC):

```
1> SELECT TOP 10  LastName, FirstName
2> FROM Person.Person
3> ORDER BY LastName
4> GO

LastName                                              FirstName
---------------------------------------------------  ---------
Abbas                                                 Syed
Abel                                                  Catherine
Abercrombie                                           Kim
Abercrombie                                           Kim
Abercrombie                                           Kim
Abolrous                                              Hazem
Abolrous                                              Sam
Acevedo                                               Humberto
Achong                                                Gustavo
Ackerman                                              Pilar

(10 rows affected)
```

As you can see, the default form of order is ascending (ASC), and if you want the descending form you will need to specify the keyword DESC. In addition to simple sorting by one column, sorting can be carried out on multiple columns where each can have a different form of sorting:

```
1> SELECT TOP 10  LastName, FirstName
2> FROM Person.Person
3> ORDER BY LastName DESC, FirstName ASC
4> GO
```

LastName	FirstName
Zwilling	Michael
Zwilling	Michael
Zukowski	Jake
Zugelder	Judy
Zubaty	Carla
Zubaty	Patricia
Zimprich	Karin
Zimprich	Karin
Zimmerman	Bianca
Zimmerman	Candice

```
(10 rows affected)
```

While formatting data output, in many cases you will be required to include some sort of mathematical operator, such as addition, multiplication, subtraction, and so on. Mathematical expressions can be used in SELECT and WHERE clauses, and are very useful for creating more descriptive results and eliminating the necessity for data adjustment after the query results have been delivered:

```
1> SELECT ProductNumber AS Number,
2> ListPrice AS 'Old price',
3> (ListPrice*1.17) AS 'New price'
4> FROM Production.Product
5> WHERE ListPrice > 3400
6> GO
```

Number	Old price	New price
BK-R93R-62	3578.2700	4186.575900
BK-R93R-44	3578.2700	4186.575900
BK-R93R-48	3578.2700	4186.575900
BK-R93R-52	3578.2700	4186.575900
BK-R93R-56	3578.2700	4186.575900

```
(5 rows affected)
```

Overview of aggregate functions

Data summarizing is one of the most common scenarios for SQL use in business environments. It is also very important for developers, report creators, and information workers. SQL Server has several built-in aggregate functions, such as AVG, SU, and MIN, to perform summarizing data operations. Basically, those operations are taken using multiple values to produce a single (scalar) value (for example, the average function on a column with 10,000 values will always produce a single output):

Function	Example	Description
MIN	MIN (ListPrice)	Finds the smallest value in a column
MAX	MAX (Grade)	Finds the largest values in a column
SUM	SUM (TotalSales)	Creates a sum of numeric values in a column (non-null)
AVG	AVG (Size)	Creates an average of numeric values in a column (non-null)
COUNT	COUNT (OrderID) COUNT (*)	COUNT with column name counts the number of data and ignores nulls COUNT (*) counts the number of rows in the table

The following query uses four out of five aggregate functions to search the Production.Product table to find the largest and smallest list prices, the average size of all products, and the total days spent to manufacture all products:

```
1> SELECT MAX (ListPrice) AS MaxPrice,
2> MIN (ListPrice) AS MinPrice,
3> AVG (CONVERT (int, Size)) AS AvgSize,
4> SUM (DaysToManufacture) AS TotalDays
5> FROM Production.Product
6> WHERE ISNUMERIC (Size) = 1
7> GO

MaxPrice                MinPrice                AvgSize       TotalDays
--------------------    --------------------    -----------   -----------
3578,27                 54,99                   48            474

(1 row(s) affected))
```

Notice that, before calculating the average value on Size, we need to convert the data using CONVERT to numeric data type.

Aggregate functions and NULL values

Most queries with aggregation functions inside ignore NULL values. This can produce anomalies in result sets and create confusion. The following query will count the number of rows and number of column data in the `Production.Product` table:

```
1> SELECT COUNT (*), COUNT (SellEndDate)
2> FROM Production.Product
3> GO
```

```
----------- -----------
504         98
Warning: Null value is eliminated by an aggregate or other SET operation.

(1 row(s) affected)
```

- COUNT (*): Counts all records in a table including records with NULL and duplicate values.
- COUNT (SellEndDate): Ignores NULL values. You can't count something that is UNKNOWN (NULL).

GROUP BY clause

Often, we find it useful to group data by some characteristic of the group, such as department or division, or benefit level, so that summary statistics about the group (totals, averages, and so on) can be calculated. For example, to calculate the average student grades, the user could group the grades of all students. The GROUP BY clause is used to divide the rows of a table into groups that have matching values in one or more columns.

First, let's examine the following example and error that it produces.

We want a list of all products, with a count of sales items for specific products and profit information. The query looks just fine; so, then, what is the problem? The problem is that COUNT and SUM returns a single (scalar) value, and the first column in SELECT (ProductID) returns all products. So, we have a conflict in result sets. The solution for this is to use the GROUP BY clause:

```
1> SELECT ProductID, COUNT (ProductID) AS ProductSales,
2> SUM (LineTotal) As Profit
3> FROM Purchasing.PurchaseOrderDetail
4> ORDER BY ProductID
5> GO
```

```
Msg 8120, Level 16, State 1, Line 1
Column 'Purchasing.PurchaseOrderDetail.ProductID' is invalid in the select
list because it is not contained in either an aggregate function or the
GROUP BY clause.
```

Now let's modify this example and run it again:

```
1> SELECT TOP 5 ProductID, COUNT (ProductID) AS ProductSales,
2> SUM (LineTotal) As Profit
3> FROM Purchasing.PurchaseOrderDetail
4> GROUP BY ProductID
5> ORDER BY ProductID
6> GO

ProductID    ProductSales Profit
-----------  ------------ --------------------
1            51           7740,565
2            50           6287,40
4            51           8724,9015
317          80           1246014,00
318          80           1532916,00

(5 row(s) affected)
```

The explanation is quite simple. In our case, GROUPY BY ProductID creates groups of unique data in the result set based on data in column ProductID; for example, if it finds the same ProductID in 10 places, GROUP BY takes the group representative and the others are grouped. Then, for each group, it makes an aggregation.

HAVING clause

The HAVING clause was added to SQL because the WHERE keyword could not be used with aggregate functions and would result in the error seen in the following example.

Before we explain HAVING, let's go back for a moment on the WHERE clause and combine it with aggregations:

```
1> SELECT SUM (OrderQty) AS TotalOrderQty
2> FROM Purchasing.PurchaseOrderDetail
3> WHERE SUM (OrderQty) > 1000
4> GO
Msg 147, Level 15, State 1, Line 1
An aggregate may not appear in the WHERE clause unless it is in a subquery
contained in a HAVING clause or a select list, and the column being
aggregated is an outer reference.
```

This error means that we cannot use aggregation in a WHERE clause. HAVING allows you to define a search parameter similar to WHERE, but in this case HAVING can handle groups returned by the GROUP BY clause as seen in the following example:

```
1> SELECT SUM (OrderQty) AS TotalOrderQty
2> FROM Purchasing.PurchaseOrderDetail
3> HAVING SUM (OrderQty) > 1000
4> GO

TotalOrderQty
-------------
2348637

(1 row(s) affected
```

JOIN operators

Queries created on a single table can sometimes provide you with the necessary data. However, in practice, most queries require data that is acquired from multiple tables. To create a query that will combine data from multiple tables into a single result set requires you to use a powerful relational operator called JOIN:

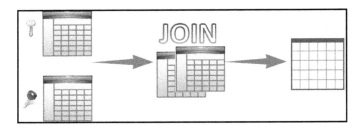

Figure 6-1. Two table join operation

The JOIN operator provides you with the functionality to combine data from two or more tables into a single result set. Related tables are created with common columns, usually named primary and foreign key. These keys are used to join related tables to each other.

The database engine performs table joins in a way that it takes the record from the left table and, usually based on the common field, checks for one or more matches in the right table. There are several types of JOIN operators, but the most common ones are INNER JOIN and OUTER JOIN.

INNER JOIN

An INNER JOIN can be viewed as a cross-section of two sets. Therefore, when you create an INNER JOIN with two tables, depending on the conditions of connectivity, the resulting set will contain only those elements that are common to both tables. In other words, an INNER JOIN matches rows from two tables based on the common columns values in each table. In other words, an INNER JOIN matches rows from two tables based on the common columns values in each table.

The following query will create a list of all products for which a review is created. Since the products and reviews data are stored in two separate tables, this is a signal for the JOIN operator:

```
1> SELECT P.ProductNumber, LEFT (R.Comments, 20)
2> FROM Production.Product AS P
3> INNER JOIN Production.ProductReview AS R
4> ON P.ProductID = R.ProductID
5> GO

ProductNumber                   Comments
----------------------------    --------------------
SO-B909-M                       I can't believe I'm
PD-M562                         A little on the heav
PD-M562                         Maybe it's just beca
BK-R64Y-40                      The Road-550-W from

(4 rows affected)
```

 I am using the string function LEFT because the comments are large and don't fit in readable form in the console window.

As you can see, the Product table contains 504 rows, and the table ProductReview only 4. However, since we have used INNER JOIN, the result set will consist of those rows that match both tables. Table joining is made based on the value of the ProductID column which we specified by using the ON operator. It is also important to note the way in which we have used aliases, and based on them we have referenced columns in different tables. As an exercise, try to make the previous example without using aliases. Since INNER JOIN is the default type of join, you can simply use the keyword JOIN.

OUTER JOIN

An OUTER JOIN will return all rows that exist in the left table, even though corresponding rows do not exist in the right table. Therefore, OUTER JOIN enables you to create a result set that includes even the data that does not have a match in the joining table, and in the place of a matching value they will be assigned a NULL. There are two common variations of OUTER JOIN operator: LEFT and RIGHT.

The result set of a LEFT OUTER JOIN includes all the rows from the left table and only the matching rows from the right table.

Here is a just a little-modified version of the previous example with LEFT JOIN operator:

```
1> SELECT TOP 7 P.ProductNumber, LEFT (R.Comments, 20)
2> FROM Production.Product AS P
3> LEFT JOIN Production.ProductReview AS R
4> ON P.ProductID = R.ProductID
5> ORDER BY R.Comments DESC
6> GO
```

```
ProductNumber                  Comments
------------------------       -----------------------
BK-R64Y-40                     The Road-550-W from...
PD-M562                        Maybe it's just beca...
SO-B909-M                      I can't believe I'm...
PD-M562                        A little on the heav...
CR-7833                        NULL
CN-6137                        NULL
CB-2903                        NULL

(10 rows affected)
```

A RIGHT OUTER JOIN is the reverse of a LEFT OUTER JOIN and therefore it includes all the rows from the right table and only the matching rows from the left table, which is in this case the same as the result of the INNER JOIN. In the other words, there is no review for products that do not exist in the left table:

```
1> SELECT TOP 10 P.ProductNumber, LEFT (R.Comments, 20)
2> FROM Production.Product AS P
3> RIGHT JOIN Production.ProductReview AS R
4> ON P.ProductID = R.ProductID
5> GO
```

```
ProductNumber
------------------------       --------------------
SO-B909-M                      I can't believe I'm
```

```
PD-M562                        A little on the heav
PD-M562                        Maybe it's just beca
BK-R64Y-40                     The Road-550-W from
```

```
(4 rows affected)
```

Multiple joins

Generating detailed information about an entity in a single result set will often require data from multiple tables. This means you will have to apply a corresponding type of JOIN on more than two tables.

The next query will collect information on the quantity of every product on each production location. The required data are located in three different tables: Product (contains data about products), ProductInventory (contains data about the quantity of every product on each location), and Location (contains data about the location of production). It is important to note which common columns or keys are used to join tables:

```
1> SELECT TOP 10 P.Name AS Product, L.Name AS Location, I.Quantity
2> FROM Production.Product AS P
3> INNER JOIN Production.ProductInventory AS I
4> ON P.ProductID = I.ProductID
5> INNER JOIN Production.Location L
6> ON L.LocationID = I.LocationID
7> ORDER BY Quantity DESC
8> GO
```

Product	Location	Quantity
Seat Lug	Miscellaneous Storage	924
Hex Nut 7	Miscellaneous Storage	897
Spokes	Miscellaneous Storage	888
Hex Nut 14	Miscellaneous Storage	780
Hex Nut 19	Subassembly	763
Seat Lug	Final Assembly	729
Touring Rim	Subassembly	724
Seat Stays	Miscellaneous Storage	715
Hex Nut 10	Miscellaneous Storage	710
Spokes	Subassembly	702

```
(10 rows affected)
```

If you want to narrow the search to a specific location and quantity, it is necessary to define the search conditions in the WHERE clause. For example:

```
WHERE L.Name = 'Tool Crib' AND I.Quantity < 200
```

As a special form of JOIN we can consider self-join, which refers to any kind of join used to join a table to itself. Self-join is used in cases where the inner and outer queries refer to the same table. The following query example will return only those products with a price that is higher than the average prices of the same sub-category:

```
1> SELECT TOP 4 P1.Name, P1.ListPrice
2> FROM Production.Product AS P1
3> INNER JOIN Production.Product AS P2
4> ON P1.ProductSubcategoryID = P2.ProductSubcategoryID
5> GROUP BY P1.Name, P1.ListPrice
6> HAVING P1.ListPrice > AVG (P2.ListPrice)
7> GO
```

```
Name                                     ListPrice
---------------------------------------  ----------
Mountain-100 Silver, 38                    3399.9900
Mountain-100 Silver, 42                    3399.9900
Mountain-100 Silver, 44                    3399.9900
Mountain-100 Silver, 48                    3399.9900

(5 rows affected)
```

Summary

You should now have sufficient skills to recognize scenarios that require the use of aggregations based on AVG, SUM, COUNT, and other set-based functions. You'll also have an understanding of the GROUP BY clause, and filtering result sets with HAVING. Also, you should be able to create queries that can be used to support the basic forms of reporting. The database typically contains dozens of tables, and it is therefore extremely important that you master creating queries over multiple tables. This includes knowledge of the functioning JOIN operators with a combination of elements of string manipulation. This chapter completes this aspect of SQL Server on Linux.

In the next chapter, we will cover topics relevant for administration and database operations.

7
Backup and Recovery Operations

Do you have a backup? Yes! How often do you take backups? We have a backup of our database from the day of installation, so we can restore it to the initial state. *Sorry, you don't have any backups*. I don't know about you, but this scenario is so common that it scares me. Believe me, this hypnotic conversation can be heard even in large companies.

When it comes to a database, backups are something that you should consider and reconsider really carefully. Mistakes can cost you: money, users, data, and time, each of which can have bigger consequences. **Backup** and **restore** are elements of a much wider picture known as **disaster recovery** and it is a science itself. However, these two operations are the foundation for everything else.

In this chapter, you will learn:

- SQL Server recovery models
- How transaction log works
- Elements of backup strategy
- Backup and restore

SQL Server recovery models

Before you even think about your backups, you need to understand the recovery models that SQL Server internally uses while the database is in operational mode. A recovery model is about maintaining data in the event of a server failure. Also, it defines the amount of information that SQL Server writes to the log file for the purpose of recovery.

SQL Server has three database recovery models:

- Simple recovery model
- Full recovery model
- Bulk-logged recovery model

Simple recovery model

This model is typically used for small databases and scenarios where data changes are infrequent. It is limited to restoring the database to the point when the last backup was created. It means that all changes made after the backup are lost. You will need to recreate all changes manually. The major benefit of this model is that the log file takes only a small amount of storage space. How and when to use it depends on the business scenario.

Full recovery model

This model is recommended when recovery from damaged storage is the highest priority and data loss should be minimal. SQL Server uses copies of database and log files to restore the database. The database engine logs all changes to the database, including bulk operation and most DDL statements.

If the transaction log file is not damaged, SQL Server can recover all data except any transaction which are in process at the time of failure (that is, not committed in to the database file). All logged transactions give you the opportunity of point-in-time recovery, which is a really cool feature.

A major limitation of this model is the large size of the log files which leads you to performance and storage issues. Use it only in scenarios where every insert is important and loss of data is not an option.

Bulk-logged recovery model

This model is somewhere between simple and full. It uses database and log backups to recreate the database. Compared to the full recovery model, it uses less log space for CREATE INDEX and bulk load operations, such as SELECT INTO. Let's look at this example. SELECT INTO can load a table with 1,000,000 records with a single statement. The log will only record the occurrence of these operations but not the details. This approach uses less storage space compared to the full recovery model.

The bulk-logged recovery model is good for databases which are used for ETL process and data migrations.

As you know from Chapter 6, *A Crash Course in Querying*, SQL Server has a system database model. This database is the template for each new one you create. If you use only the CREATE DATABASE statement without any additional parameters, it simply copies the model database with all the properties and metadata. It also inherits the default recovery model, which is full. So, the conclusion is that each new database will be in full recovery mode. This can be changed during and after the creation process.

Here is a SQL statement to check recovery models of all your databases on SQL Server on Linux instance:

```
1> SELECT name, recovery_model, recovery_model_desc
2> FROM sys.databases
3> GO

name                     recovery_model recovery_model_desc
------------------------ -------------- -------------------
master                                3 SIMPLE
tempdb                                3 SIMPLE
model                                 1 FULL
msdb                                  3 SIMPLE
AdventureWorks                        3 SIMPLE
WideWorldImporters                    3 SIMPLE

(6 rows affected)
```

The following DDL statement will change the recovery model for the model database from full to simple:

```
1> USE master
2> ALTER DATABASE model
3> SET RECOVERY SIMPLE
4> GO
```

If you now execute the SELECT statement again to check recovery models, you will notice that model now has different properties.

How transaction log works

If you are Linux user with MySQL and PostgreSQL experience, you have probably noticed that SQL Server works with two types of files, `.data` and `.log`:

- `data`: A container file for database objects and data itself
- `log`: A container file for logging database operations, depending on recovery model

Each database has at least one data and log file. However, based on business needs, this number can be larger.

The transaction log file is the heart of **Atomicity, Consistency, Integrity, and Durability** (**ACID**). Those four magic words are the most powerful tools of every relational database. In a nutshell, it helps that, if something goes wrong during the business process, all changes are written to the database or returned to the state prior to the transaction. ACID in SQL Server is implemented through **Write Ahead Log** (**WAL**). The following figure describes that process:

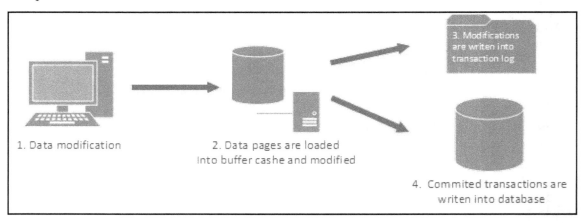

Figure 7-1 WAL process in SQL Server

As you see, all changes are made first on the memory level and written to the log file. After the transaction is committed, changes are written to the data file. This process ensures that no changes will be partially committed. Relational databases are all or nothing.

Elements of backup strategy

A good backup strategy is not just about creating a backup. This is a process of many elements and conditions that should be filed to achieve the final goal, and this is the most efficient backup strategy plan. To create a good strategy, we need to analyze the following:

- Who can create backups?
- Backup media
- Types of backup

Who can create backups?

This issue is part of the security subject, and that is covered in Chapter 8, *User Management*. For now, let's just say that a SQL Server user who is authorized to execute backup operations needs to have a security role. Security roles are:

- **sysadmin** server role: Every user with sysadmin permission can work with backups. Our default sa user is a member of the sysadmin role.
- **db_owner** database role: Any user who can create databases by default can execute any backup/restore operations.
- **db_backupoperator** database role: Sometimes you need just one person to deal with every aspect of backup operations. This is common for large scale organizations with tens or even hundreds of SQL Server instances. In those environments, backup is not a trivial business.

Backup media

An important decision is where to store backup files and how to organize backup files and devices. SQL Server gives you a large set of combinations to define your own backup media strategy. Before we explain how to store backups, let's describe the following terms:

- **Backup disk** is a hard disk or other storage device that contains backup files. Backup file is just an ordinary file on the top of the filesystem.
- **Media set** is a collection of backup media which are in an ordered way and fixed type. For example, three types of devices Tape1, Tape2, and Tape3.

- **Physical backup device** can be a disk file or tape drive. You will need to provide information to SQL Server about your backup device. A backup file that is created before it is used for a backup operation is called a backup device.

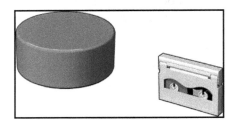

Figure 7-2 Backup devices

The simplest way to store and handle database backups is by using a back disk and storing them as regular operating system files. Usually, with extension `.bak`, Linux does not much care about the extension, but it is a good practice to mark those files with something obvious.

This chapter will explain how to use backup disk devices because every reader of this book should have a hard disk with the installation of SQL Server on Linux. Tapes and media sets are used for the majority of database operations, such as enterprise class business (banks, government institutions, and so on).

A disk backup device can be anything from a simple hard disk drive, SSD disk, hot-swap disk, USB drive, and so on. The size of the disk determines the maximum size of the database backup file.

It is recommended that you use a different disk for backup. Using this approach, you will separate database data and log disks.
Imagine this: database files and backups are on the same device. If that device fails your perfect backup strategy will fall like a tower of cards. Always separate them. Some serious disaster recovery strategies (backup is only smart part of it) suggest using different geographic locations. This makes sense: a natural disaster can knock out a business if you can't restore your system from a secondary location in a reasonable amount of time.

Types of backup

SQL Server gives you several methods to back up your databases based on your business scenarios and needs. The first three are the most common ones and I will explain them:

- Full database backups
- Transaction log backups
- Differential backups
- Partial backups
- Tail-log backups
- File or filegroup backups
- Copy-only backups

Full database backups

A full backup of a database includes all data files and active parts of a transaction log. A full backup represents the database at the time of the backup and represents the baseline in the event of a system failure. This type of backup is the foundation for other types, such as differential, transaction log, and is a good starting point for planning a backup strategy. In most case scenarios, a full database backup is not enough to prevent data loss. The only case when this is not true is when you use a database in read-only mode.

An example of a full backup strategy is shown in the following figure:

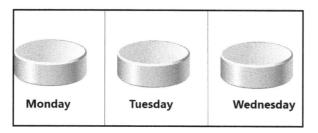

Figure 7-3 Full backup strategy

This picture represents an example of when full backup is created every 24 hours; let's say, at midnight. The problem with this example arises if your system experiences failures at, say, 3pm the next day: then you will have 15 hours of lost data. This could equate to 10 records or 10 million records.

Transaction log backups

This type of backup records all database modifications by backing-up log records. They are generally much smaller than full database backups. Pre-requirements are at least one full database backup and full recovery mode of database. We can set the log backup for every 15 minutes or less, depending on your business needs. This strategy is necessary for point-in-time recovery.

An example of a transaction backup strategy is shown in the following figure:

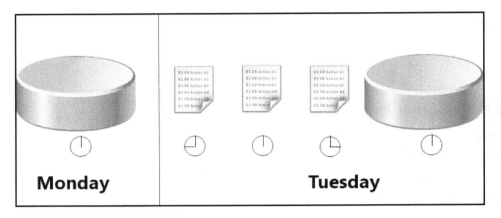

Figure 7-4 Transaction log backup strategy

This example illustrates scenarios when a full database is taken every day at midnight, and logs backup every 3 hours between full backups. In this case, you can restore any transaction from log backups. First, you need to restore full database backups and every log backup until you reach a point in time that suits you. A side effect is that you can have a large number of small backups. Imagine that you create a log backup every 15 minutes.

Differential backups

The problem with transaction backups can be minimized with differential backup. This type of backup is used to save data changes between the last full and differential backup. It is based on data files. The important thing to remember is that differential backup is not possible without full backup. Also, it minimizes the time that is necessary for restoring a frequently modified database. For example, if a full database backup file is 2 GB and you have only 10 MB of changes after, the differential backup is just an additional 10 MB (differential).

An example of a differential backup strategy is shown in the following figure:

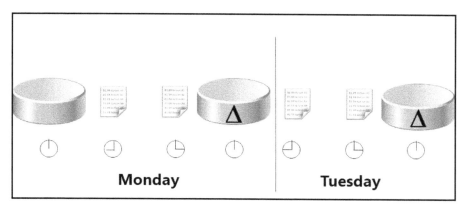

Figure 7-5 Differential backup strategy

The previous scenario represents full database backup at midnight, daily. In between, we have our log backups every three hours and a differential every day at noon. This approach drastically reduces the number of restore operations because a differential backup contains all changes from the last full database backup. If your system experiences a failure at 3.15pm then you need to restore one full, one differential, and one transaction log backup. This is the most efficient data loss prevention strategy.

Backup and restore

Now it's time for SQL coding and implementing backup/restore operations in our own environments. We will use the University database that you created in Chapter 4, *Database in the Sandbox:*

1. First let's create a full database backup of our University database:

```
1> BACKUP DATABASE University
2> TO DISK = '/var/opt/mssql/data/University.bak'
3> GO
Processed 376 pages for database'University', file 'University' on
file 1.
Processed 7 pages for database 'University', file 'University_log'
on file 1.
BACKUP DATABASE successfully processed 383 pages in 0.562 seconds
(5.324 MB/sec)
```

2. Now let's check the content of the table `Students`:

```
1> USE University
2> GO
Changed database context to 'University'
1> SELECT LastName, FirstName
2> FROM Students
3> GO
LastName          FirstName
----------------  ----------
Azemovic          Imran
Avdic             Selver
Azemovic          Sara
Doe               John
(4 rows affected)
```

3. As you can see there are four records. Let's now simulate a large import from the `AdventureWorks` database, `Person.Person` table. We will adjust the `PhoneNumber` data to fit our 13 nvarchar characters. But first we will drop unique index `UQ_user_name` so that we can quickly import a large amount of data.

```
1> DROP INDEX UQ_user_name
2> ON dbo.Students
3> GO
```

```
1> INSERT INTO Students (LastName, FirstName, Email, Phone, UserName)
2> SELECT T1.LastName, T1.FirstName, T2.PhoneNumber, NULL, 'user.name'
3> FROM AdventureWorks.Person.Person AS T1
4> INNER JOIN AdventureWorks.Person.PersonPhone AS T2
5> ON T1.BusinessEntityID = T2.BusinessEntityID
6> WHERE LEN (T2.PhoneNumber) < 13
7> AND LEN (T1.LastName) < 15 AND LEN (T1.FirstName)< 10
8> GO
(10661 rows affected)
```

4. Let's check the new row numbers:

```
1> SELECT COUNT (*) FROM Students
2> GO
-----------
10665
(1 rows affected)
```

As you see the table now has 10,665 rows (10,661+4). But don't forget that we had created a full database backup before the import procedure.

5. Now, we will create a differential backup of the `University` database:

```
1> BACKUP DATABASE University
2> TO DISK = '/var/opt/mssql/data/University-diff.bak'
3> WITH DIFFERENTIAL
4> GO
Processed 216 pages for database 'University', file 'University' on
file 1.
Processed 3 pages for database 'University', file 'University_log'
on file 1.
BACKUP DATABASE WITH DIFFERENTIAL successfully processed 219 pages
in 0.365 seconds (4.676 MB/sec).
```

6. If you want to see the state of `.bak` files on the disk, follow this procedure. However, first enter super user mode with `sudo su`. This is necessary because a regular user does not have access to the `data` folder:

Figure 7-6 University database backup files

7. Now let's test the transaction log backup of `University` database log file. However, first you will need to make some changes inside the `Students` table:

```
1> UPDATE Students
2> SET Phone = 'N/A'
3> WHERE Phone IS NULL
4> GO
1> BACKUP LOG University
2> TO DISK = '/var/opt/mssql/data/University-log.bak'
3> GO
Processed 501 pages for database 'University', file
```

```
'University_log' on file 1.
        BACKUP LOG successfully processed 501 pages in 0.620 seconds (6.313
MB/sec).
```

Next steps are to test restore database options of full and differential backup procedures.

8. First, restore the full database backup of University database. Remember that the Students table had four records before first backup, and it currently has 10,665 (as we checked in *step 4*):

```
1> ALTER DATABASE University
2> SET SINGLE_USER WITH ROLLBACK IMMEDIATE
3> RESTORE DATABASE University
4> FROM DISK = '/var/opt/mssql/data/University.bak'
5> WITH REPLACE
6> ALTER DATABASE University SET MULTI_USER
7> GO
Nonqualified transactions are being rolled back. Estimated rollback
completion: 0%.
Nonqualified transactions are being rolled back. Estimated rollback
completion: 100%.
        Processed 376 pages for database 'University', file 'University' on
file 1.
        Processed 7 pages for database 'University', file 'University_log'
on file 1.
        RESTORE DATABASE successfully processed 383 pages in 0.520 seconds
(5.754 MB/sec).
```

Before the restore procedure, the database is switched to single user mode. This way we are closing all connections that could abort the restore procedure. In the last step, we are switching the database to multi-user mode again.

9. Let's check the number of rows again. You will see the database is restored to its initial state, before the import of more than 10,000 records from the AdventureWorks database:

```
1> SELECT COUNT (*) FROM Students
2> GO
-------
      4
(1 rows affected)
```

10. Now it's time to restore the content of the differential backup and return the
University database to its state after the import procedure:

```
1> USE master
2> ALTER DATABASE University
3> SET SINGLE_USER WITH ROLLBACK IMMEDIATE
4> RESTORE DATABASE University
5> FROM DISK = N'/var/opt/mssql/data/University.bak'
6> WITH FILE = 1, NORECOVERY, NOUNLOAD, REPLACE, STATS = 5
7> RESTORE DATABASE University
8> FROM DISK = N'/var/opt/mssql/data/University-diff.bak'
9> WITH FILE = 1, NOUNLOAD, STATS = 5
10> ALTER DATABASE University SET MULTI_USER
11> GO
Processed 376 pages for database 'University', file 'University' on
file 1.
Processed 7 pages for database 'University', file 'University_log'
on file 1.
RESTORE DATABASE successfully processed 383 pages in 0.529 seconds
(5.656 MB/sec).
Processed 216 pages for database 'University', file 'University' on
file 1.
Processed 3 pages for database 'University', file 'University_log'
on file 1.
RESTORE DATABASE successfully processed 219 pages in 0.309 seconds
(5.524 MB/sec).
```

In the final part of this chapter, we'll look at a really cool feature of SQL Server: **backup compression**. A backup can be a very large file, and if companies create backups on daily basis, then you can do the math on the amount of storage required.

Disk space is cheap today, but it is not free. As a database administrator on SQL Server on Linux, you should consider any possible option to optimize and save money. Backup compression is just that kind of feature. It provides you with a compression procedure (ZIP, RAR) after creating regular backups. So, you save time, space, and money.

Let's consider a full database backup of the University database. The uncompressed file is about 3 MB. After we create a new one with compression, the size should be reduced. The compression ratio mostly depends on data types inside the database. It is not a magic stick but it can save space.

The following SQL command will create a full database backup of the University database and compress it:

```
1> BACKUP DATABASE University
2> TO DISK = '/var/opt/mssql/data/University-compress.bak'
3> WITH NOFORMAT, INIT, SKIP, NOREWIND, NOUNLOAD, COMPRESSION, STATS = 10
4> GO
```

Now exit to bash, enter super user mode, and type the following `ls` command to compare the size of the backup files:

```
tumbleweed:/home/dba # ls -lh /var/opt/mssql/data/U*.bak
```

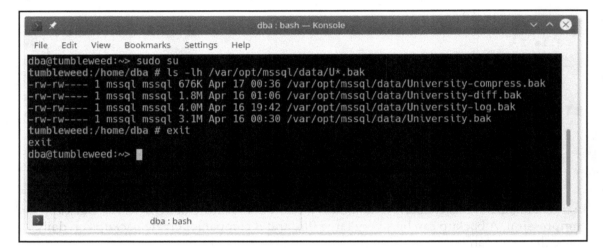

Figure 7-7 University database backup files

As you can see, the compression size is 676 KB and it is around five times smaller. That is a huge space saving without any additional tools. SQL Server on Linux has one security feature with backup, and that will be elaborated in `Chapter 9`, *Implementing Data Protection*.

Summary

This chapter has walked you through some important options. Backup and restore is not something that you can leave aside. It requires serious analysis and planning, and SQL Server gives you powerful backup types and options to create your disaster recovery policy on SQL Server on Linux. You can do some additional research and expand your knowledge. A good starting point is the official SQL Server on Linux online documentation.

8
User Management

Today, security is a hot topic. Mistakes can come at a high price, and lead to the loss of customers and business. Almost every day, we hear about some serious data breach. User management is the first point at which the security story actually begins.

SQL Server has a very powerful mechanism for checking user identity. Based on that process, we can configure all other aspects of security from the higher (server) to the lower (database) level.

In this chapter, we will go into more detail about the process of authentication, and authorization, and how to gain access to concrete SQL Server assets (also known as securables).

In this chapter, you will learn the following:

- The authentication process
- The authorization process
- Accessing SQL Server resources
- Schema separation

Authentication process

This question is very simple: *Who are you?* Unfortunately, the answer is not so simple. The database engine needs to verify your identity, and I believe a more important question is *Is this really you?*

During the setup procedure, you have to select a sa password which actually uses the SQL Server authentication process. This database engine comes from Windows and it is tightly connected with Active Directory and internal Windows authentication. In this phase of development, SQL Server on Linux only supports SQL authentication.

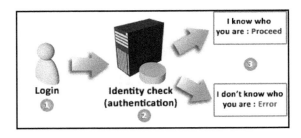

Figure 8-1. Authentication process

SQL Server has a very secure entry point. This means no access without the correct credentials. Every information system has some way of checking a user's identity, but SQL Server has three different ways of verifying identity, and the ability to select the most appropriate method, based on individual or business needs.

When using SQL Server authentication, logins are created on SQL Server. Both the user name and the password are created by using SQL Server and stored in SQL Server. Users connecting through SQL Server authentication must provide their credentials every time that they connect (user name and password are transmitted through the network).

 When using SQL Server authentication, it is highly recommended to set strong passwords for all SQL Server accounts.

As you'll have noticed, so far you have not had any problems accessing SQL Server resources. The reason for this is very simple. You are working under the sa login. This login has unlimited SQL Server access. In some real-life scenarios, sa is not something to play with. It is good practice to create a login under a different name with the same level of access.

Now let's see how to create a new SQL Server login. But, first, we'll check the list of current SQL Server logins. To do this, access the `sys.sql_logins` system catalog view and three attributes: `name`, `is_policy_checked`, and `is_expiration_checked`. The attribute `name` is clear; the second one will show the login enforcement password policy; and the third one is for enforcing account expiration. Both attributes have a Boolean type of value: `TRUE` or `FALSE` (1 or 0).

1. Type the following command to list all SQL logins:

```
1> SELECT name, is_policy_checked, is_expiration_checked
2> FROM sys.sql_logins
3> WHERE name = 'sa'
4> GO
name                 is_policy_checked is_expiration_checked
---------------      ----------------- ---------------------
sa                               1                          0
(1 rows affected)
```

2. If you want to see what your password for the sa login looks like, just type this version of the same statement. This is the result of the hash function:

```
1> SELECT password_hash
2> FROM sys.sql_logins
3> WHERE name = 'sa'
4> GO
password_hash
-----------------------------------------------------------
0x0200110F90F4F4057F1DF84B2CCB42861AE469B2D43E27B3541628
B72F72588D36B8E0DDF879B5C0A87FD2CA6ABCB7284CDD0871
B07C58D0884DFAB11831AB896B9EEE8E7896
(1 rows affected)
```

3. Now let's create the login dba, which will require a strong password and will not expire:

```
1> USE master
2> GO
Changed database context to 'master'.
1> CREATE LOGIN dba
2> WITH PASSWORD ='S0m3c00lPa$$',
3> CHECK_EXPIRATION = OFF,
4> CHECK_POLICY = ON
5> GO
```

4. Re-check the dba on the login list:

```
1> SELECT name, is_policy_checked, is_expiration_checked
2> FROM sys.sql_logins
3> WHERE name = 'dba'
4> GO
name                    is_policy_checked is_expiration_checked
-----------------       ----------------- ---------------------
dba                                     1                     0
(1 rows affected)
```

Notice that dba logins do not have any kind of privilege. Let's check that part. First close your current sqlcmd session by typing `exit`. Now, connect again but, instead of using sa, you will connect with the dba login. After the connection has been successfully created, try to change the content of the active database to `AdventureWorks`. This process, based on the login name, should looks like this:

```
# dba@tumbleweed:~> sqlcmd -S suse -U dba
Password:
1> USE AdventureWorks
2> GO
Msg 916, Level 14, State 1, Server tumbleweed, Line 1
The server principal "dba" is not able to access the database
"AdventureWorks" under the current security context.
```

As you can see, the authentication process will not grant you anything. Simply, you can enter the building but you can't open any door. You will need to pass the process of authorization first.

Authorization process

After authenticating a user, SQL Server will then determine whether the user has permission to view and/or update data, view metadata, or perform administrative tasks (server-side level, database-side level, or both). If the user, or a group to which the user is a member, has some type of permission within the instance and/or specific databases, SQL Server will let the user connect.

In a nutshell, authorization is the process of checking user access rights to specific securables. In this phase, SQL Server will check the login policy to determine whether there are any access rights to the server and/or database level. Login can have successful authentication, but no access to the securables. This means that authentication is just one step before login can proceed with any action on SQL Server.

SQL Server will check the authorization process on every T-SQL statement. In other words, if a user has SELECT permissions on some database, SQL Server will not check once and then forget until the next authentication/authorization process. Every statement will be verified by the policy to determine whether there are any changes.

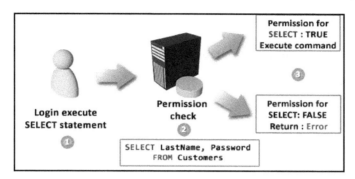

Figure 8-2. Authorization process

Permissions are the set of rules that govern the level of access that principals have to securables. Permissions in an SQL Server system can be granted, revoked, or denied. Each of the SQL Server securables has associated permissions that can be granted to each principal.

The only way a principal can access a resource in an SQL Server system is if it is granted permission to do so, as you can see in *Figure 8-2*. At this point, it is important to note that authentication and authorization are two different processes, but they work in conjunction with one another. Furthermore, the terms **login** and **user** are to be used very carefully, as they are not the same:

- Login is the authentication part
- User is the authorization part

Prior to accessing any database on SQL Server, the login needs to be mapped as a user. Each login can have one or many user instances in different databases. For example, one login can have read permission in AdventureWorks and write permission in WideWorldImporters. This type of granular security is a great SQL Server security feature. A login name can be the same or different from a user name in different databases.

In the following lines, we will create a database user dba based on login dba. The process will be based on the `AdventureWorks` database. After that we will try to enter the database and execute a `SELECT` statement on the `Person.Person` table:

```
dba@tumbleweed:~> sqlcmd -S suse -U sa
Password:
1> USE AdventureWorks
2> GO
Changed database context to 'AdventureWorks'.

1> CREATE USER dba
2> FOR LOGIN dba
3> GO
1> exit

dba@tumbleweed:~> sqlcmd -S suse -U dba
Password:
1> USE AdventureWorks
2> GO
Changed database context to 'AdventureWorks'.

1> SELECT *
2> FROM Person.Person
3> GO

Msg 229, Level 14, State 5, Server tumbleweed, Line 1
The SELECT permission was denied on the object 'Person', database
'AdventureWorks', schema 'Person'.
```

We are making progress. Now we can enter the database, but we still can't execute `SELECT` or any other SQL statement. The reason is very simple. Our dba user still is not authorized to access any types of resources.

Accessing SQL Server resources

Now that we understand the authentication/authorization process, we can create more detailed user access policies on the server and/or database level. Also, we will go into more detail about fixed server-side and database roles.

Server-level permissions

SQL Server provides nine fixed server roles. The permissions that are granted to the fixed server roles cannot be changed. You can create user-defined server roles and add server-level permissions to those roles:

- **sysadmin**: Members of the sysadmin fixed server role can perform any activity on the server.
- **serveradmin**: Members of the serveradmin fixed server role can change server-wide configuration options and shut down the server.
- **securityadmin**: Members of the securityadmin fixed server role manage logins and their properties. They can GRANT, DENY, and REVOKE server-level permissions. They can also GRANT, DENY, and REVOKE database-level permissions if they have access to a database.
- **processadmin**: Members of the processadmin fixed server role can end processes that are running in an instance of SQL Server.
- **setupadmin**: Members of the setupadmin fixed server role can add and remove linked servers.
- **bulkadmin**: Members of the bulkadmin fixed server role can run the BULK INSERT statement.
- **diskadmin**: The diskadmin fixed server role is used for managing disk files.
- **dbcreator**: Members of the dbcreator fixed server role can create, alter, drop, and restore any database.
- **public**: Every SQL Server login belongs to the public server role. When a server principal has not been granted or denied specific permissions on a securable object, the user inherits the permissions granted to public on that object.

 Only assign public permissions on any object when you want the object to be available to all users.

We can create a new SQL Server login and assign a permission to create new databases on a server with the CREATE LOGIN statement. Before you begin, don't you forget to exit the dba sqlcmd session and logon under the sa login:

```
1> USE master
2> GO
Changed database context to 'master'.

1> CREATE LOGIN dbAdmin
```

```
2> WITH PASSWORD = 'SOm3COOlPa$$',
3> CHECK_EXPIRATION = OFF,
4> CHECK_POLICY = ON
5> GO
1> ALTER SERVER ROLE dbcreator ADD MEMBER dbAdmin
2> GO
1> exit
dba@tumbleweed:~> sqlcmd -S suse -U dbAdmin
Password:
1> CREATE DATABASE TestDB
2> GO
1> USE TestDB
2> GO
Changed database context to 'TestDB'.
1> USE master
2> GO
Changed database context to 'master'.
1> DROP DATABASE TestDB
2> GO
1> exit
```

Database-level permissions

As in server-side security, database level security has a set of fixed predefined roles that incorporate any database-level task. You can combine more than one role to specify user access right in more detail:

- **db_owner**: Members of the db_owner fixed database role can perform all configuration and maintenance activities on the database, and can also drop the database
- **db_securityadmin**: Members of the db_securityadmin fixed database role can modify role membership and manage permissions
- **db_accessadmin**: Members of the db_accessadmin fixed database role can add or remove access to the database for Windows logins, Windows groups, and SQL Server logins
- **db_backupoperator**: Members of the db_backupoperator fixed database role can back up the database
- **db_ddladmin**: Members of the db_ddladmin fixed database role can run any **Data Definition Language (DDL)** command in a database
- **db_datawriter**: Members of the db_datawriter fixed database role can add, delete, or modify data in all user tables

- **db_datareader**: Members of the `db_datareader` fixed database role can read all data from all user tables
- **db_denydatawriter**: Members of the `db_denydatawriter` fixed database role cannot add, modify, or delete any data in the user tables within a database
- **db_denydatareader**: Members of the `db_denydatareader` fixed database role cannot read any data in the user tables within a database

The next example assigns two fixed database roles to the user dba, but only in the `AdventureWorks` database where this login is already mapped as user under the same name. One of the fixed database roles is the explicit read role and the other is the explicit deny role on data change:

```
1> USE AdventureWorks
2> GO
Changed database context to 'AdventureWorks'.

1> ALTER ROLE db_datareader ADD MEMBER dba
2> GO
1> ALTER ROLE db_denydatawriter ADD MEMBER dba
2> GO
```

Now log on as dba user and test these roles on your own.

Schema separation

In Microsoft SQL Server, a schema is a collection of database objects that are owned by a single principal and form a single namespace.

All objects within a schema must be uniquely named and a schema itself must be uniquely named in the database catalog. SQL Server (since version 2005) breaks the link between users and schemas. In other words, users do not own objects; schemas own objects, and principals own schemas.

Users can now have a default schema assigned using the `DEFAULT_SCHEMA` option from the `CREATE USER` and `ALTER USER` commands. If a default schema is not supplied for a user, then the dbo will be used as the default schema.

If a user from a different default schema needs to access objects in another schema, then the user will need to type a full name. For example, Denis needs to query the `Contact` tables in the `Person` schema, but he is in `Sales`. To resolve this, he would type:

SELECT * FROM Person.Contact

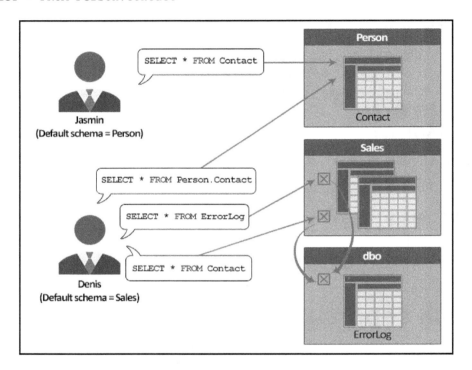

Figure 8-3. Accessing schema separated objects

Keep in mind that the default schema is dbo. When database objects are created and not explicitly put in schemas, SQL Server will assign them to the dbo default database schema. Therefore, there is no need to type dbo because it is the default schema.

Summary

In summary, understanding the basics of security and being aware of security issues contributes to an effective authentication/authorization policy. Furthermore, the precision of your permissions setting will yield a better security and permissions policy. It is important to remember that user access should be based on what they need in order to accomplish their jobs. In other words, a user's access rights should be restricted before allowing the user to access a database. It is bad practice to grant all access to a user, and then later restrict the access rights. By granting all access, you are weakening your security policy and promoting damage to the database.

Implementing Data Protection

9

Security is a hot topic today. When it comes to the database level, the consequences can be a lot bigger compared to the classic attack on network resources. This is because when all security elements fail (for instance, installation, authentication, authorization, bad access policy, and so on), all that is left is the data. In other words, if database records containing critical information are not protected, then all security elements are irrelevant.

This chapter is focused on data protection using built-in encryption features in SQL Server on Linux. If you want to prevent and minimize consequences of data breach, then this is the right chapter for you. Also, this chapter will teach you how to protect your data assets from inside threats in the form of internal malicious users.

In this chapter, you will learn the following:

- Crash course in cryptography
- Transparent Data Encryption
- Backup encryption
- Symmetric encryption
- Row-level security
- Dynamic data masking

Crash course in cryptography

We use cryptography every day: on the internet, mobile devices, ATM machines, and in almost every aspect of our digital life. In a nutshell, cryptography is about data scrambling and hiding, depending on the implementation and user-specific needs.

A database is the spine of every information system and is the specific target of potential data thieves. SQL Server has one of the best cryptographic set of features that we can use to create a state of the art security and privacy-aware systems.

Cryptography has two major terms:

- **Encryption**: The process of creating an obfuscated message from plain text using a key
- **Decryption**: The process of returning plain text from an obfuscated message using a key

From the perspective of how data is encrypted/decrypted there are two types of encryption:

- Symmetric cryptography
- Asymmetric cryptography

It's important to understand how each works and the differences between the two types. Based on that understanding, you will need to make the right decision in concrete business scenarios.

Symmetric cryptography

In symmetric cryptography cases, the sender and recipient share a key that is used to perform encryption and decryption. Symmetric cryptography is the most popular way for encryption in modern IT.

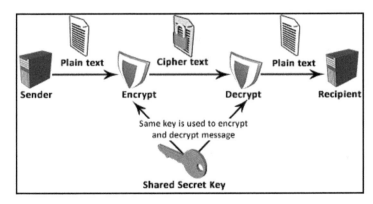

Figure 9-1. Symmetric encryption schema

Some of the most common symmetric algorithms are: Rijndael (AES) and Triple DES (3DES).

Symmetric cryptography is simple because the same key is used for encryption and decryption. However, before communication can occur, the sender and the recipient must exchange a secret key.

 The exchange of the shared secret key is the only weakness of symmetric cryptography.

Asymmetric cryptography

With asymmetric cryptography (also known as public key cryptography), the sender encrypts data with one key, and the recipient uses another key for decryption. The encryption and decryption key are known to us as a public/private key pair.

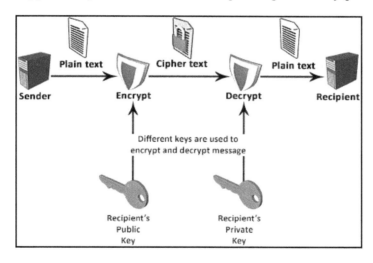

Figure 9-2. Asymmetric encryption schema

The most commonly used asymmetric algorithm is the RSA algorithm.

Asymmetric encryption requires more processing power than symmetric encryption. Because of this, asymmetric encryption is usually optimized by adding a symmetric key to encrypt a message and then asymmetrically encrypt the shared key. This can reduce the amount of data that is asymmetrically encrypted and also improves performance.

What is a key?

A key is used to configure a cryptosystem for encryption and decryption. A fundamental principle of cryptography is that the inner workings of a cryptosystem are completely known to everyone. However, the key is the only secret. This principle is known as the Kerckhoffs' principle (http://www.crypto-it.net/eng/theory/kerckhoffs.html)

From the technical perspective, a key is the product of a specific cryptosystem and is based on randomly collected information, such as random numbers, the temperature of the CPU, sample data in RAM, and so on. The randomly collected information is entered into a cryptosystem which then generates a key.

A key is hard to handle by users because it is long and contains hard readable data. Due to its complexity, a cryptosystem will associate a key with a password. In most cases, the password will trigger the key to start the encryption/decryption process.

In cryptography, the key size or length is measured in bits. A longer key means a more secure system. However, a longer key will affect performance because the encryption process takes longer. Therefore, it is important to choose an appropriate type of encryption and key length.

Both symmetric and asymmetric keys are measured in bits. Despite this similarity, symmetric and asymmetric keys are different. For example, a symmetric key using AES can be 256-bits long, while an asymmetric key using RSA can be as long as 4096 bits. Although 4096 bits may appear more secure than 256 bits, it does not mean that RSA is more secure than AES. Both RSA and AES are different and not comparable.

For example, the security available with a 1024-bit key using asymmetric RSA is considered approximately equal in security to an 80-bit key using a symmetric algorithm.

SQL Server cryptographic elements

As we've defined previously, encryption is the process of obfuscating data by the use of a key or password. This can make the data useless without the corresponding decryption key or password. Encryption does not solve access control problems. However, it enhances security by limiting data loss even if access controls are bypassed.

For example, if the database host computer is misconfigured and a hacker obtains sensitive data, that stolen information might be useless if it is encrypted.

SQL Server provides the following building blocks for the encryption; based on them you can implement all supported features, such as backup encryption, Transparent Data Encryption, column encryption and so on.

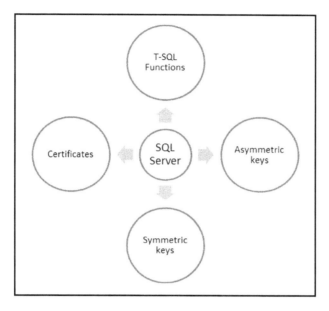

Figure 9-3. SQL Server encryption building blocks

We already know what the symmetric and asymmetric keys are. The basic concept is the same in SQL Server implementation. Later in the chapter you will practice how to create and implement all elements from the *Figure 9-3*. Let me explain the rest of the items.

T-SQL functions

SQL Server has built in support for handling encryption elements and features in the forms of T-SQL functions. You don't need any third-party software to do that, as you do with other database platforms.

Certificates

A public key certificate is a digitally-signed statement that connects the data of a public key to the identity of the person, device, or service that holds the private key. Certificates are issued and signed by a **certification authority (CA)**. You can work with self-signed certificates, but you should be careful here. This can be misused for the large set of network attacks.

SQL Server encrypts data with a hierarchical encryption. Each layer encrypts the layer beneath it using certificates, asymmetric keys, and symmetric keys.

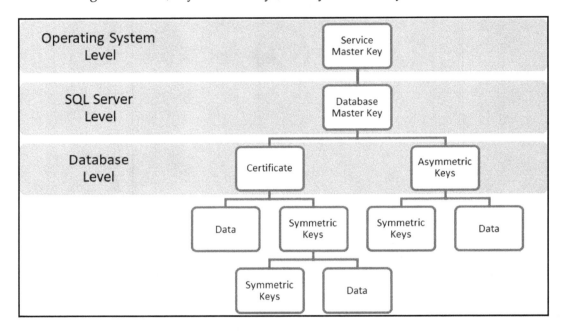

Figure 9-4. SQL Server Encryption Hierarchy

In a nutshell, *Figure 9-4* means that any key in a hierarchy is guarded (encrypted) with the key above it. In practice, if you miss just one element from the chain, decryption will be impossible. This is an important security feature, because it is really hard for an attacker to compromise all levels of security. Let me explain the most important elements in the hierarchy.

Service Master Key

SQL Server has two primary applications for keys: a **Service Master Key** (**SMK**) generated on and for a SQL Server instance, and a **database master key** (**DMK**) used for a database. The SMK is automatically generated during installation and the first time the SQL Server instance is started. It is used to encrypt the next first key in the chain.

The SMK should be backed up and stored in a secure, off-site location. This is an important step, because this is the first key in the hierarchy. Any damage at this level can prevent access to all encrypted data in the layers below. When the SMK is restored, the SQL Server decrypts all the keys and data that have been encrypted with the current SMK, and then encrypts them with the SMK from the backup.

Service Master Key can be viewed with the following system catalog view:

```
1> SELECT name, create_date
2> FROM sys.symmetric_keys
3> GO

name                       create_date
-------------------------  -------------------------
##MS_ServiceMasterKey##    2017-04-17 17:56:20.793

(1 row(s) affected)
```

Here is an example of how you can back up your SMK to the `/var/opt/mssql/backup` folder that we created in `Chapter 7`, *Backup Operations*.

> In the case that you don't have `/var/opt/mssql/backup` folder execute all 5 bash lines.
> In the case you don't have permissions to `/var/opt/mssql/backup` folder execute all lines without first one.
> ```
> # sudo mkdir /var/opt/mssql/backup
>
> # sudo chown mssql /var/opt/mssql/backup/
> # sudo chgrp mssql /var/opt/mssql/backup/
> # sudo /opt/mssql/bin/mssql-conf set
> filelocation.defaultbackupdir /var/opt/mssql/backup/
> # sudo systemctl restart mssql-server
> ```

```
1> USE master
2> GO
Changed database context to 'master'.

1> BACKUP SERVICE MASTER KEY TO FILE = '/var/opt/mssql/backup/smk'
2> ENCRYPTION BY PASSWORD = 'S0m3C001p4sw00rd'
3> --In the real scenarios your password should be more complicated
4> GO
exit
```

The next example is how to restore SMK from the backup location:

```
1> USE master
2> GO
Changed database context to 'master'.

1> RESTORE SERVICE MASTER KEY
2> FROM FILE = '/var/opt/mssql/backup/smk'
3> DECRYPTION BY PASSWORD = 'S0m3C001p4sw00rd'
4> GO
```

You can examine the contents of your SMK with the `ls` command or some internal Linux file views, such is in **Midnight Commander** (**MC**). Basically there is not much to see, but that is the power of encryption.

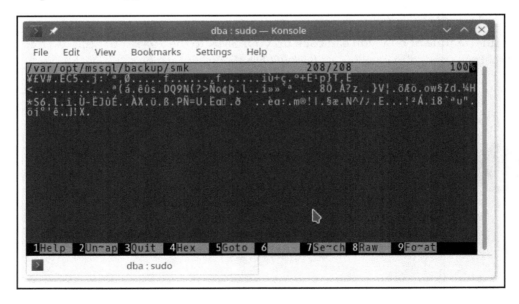

Figure 9-5. This is how SMK looks in the MC internal viewer.

The SMK is the foundation of the SQL Server encryption hierarchy. You should keep a copy at an offsite location.

Database master key

The DMK is a symmetric key used to protect the private keys of certificates and asymmetric keys that are present in the database. When it is created, the master key is encrypted by using the AES 256 algorithm and a user-supplied password. To enable the automatic decryption of the master key, a copy of the key is encrypted by using the SMK and stored in both the database (user and in the master database).

The copy stored in the master is always updated whenever the master key is changed. The next T-SQL code show how to create DMK in the Sandbox database:

```
1> CREATE DATABASE Sandbox
2> GO
1> USE Sandbox
2> GO
3> CREATE MASTER KEY
4> ENCRYPTION BY PASSWORD = 'S0m3C001p4sw00rd'
5> GO
```

Let's check where the DMK is with the sys.sysmmetric_keys system catalog view:

```
1> SELECT name, algorithm_desc
2> FROM sys.symmetric_keys
3> GO

name                         algorithm_desc
---------------------------  ----------------
##MS_DatabaseMasterKey##     AES_256

(1 row(s) affected)
```

This default can be changed by using the DROP ENCRYPTION BY SERVICE MASTER KEY option of ALTER MASTER KEY. A master key that is not encrypted by the SMK must be opened by using the OPEN MASTER KEY statement and a password.

Now that we know why the DMK is important and how to create one, we will continue with the following DMK operations:

- `ALTER`
- `OPEN`
- `CLOSE`
- `BACKUP`
- `RESTORE`
- `DROP`

These operations are important because all other encryption keys, on database-level, are dependent on the DMK.

We can easily create a new DMK for `Sandbox` and re-encrypt the keys below it in the encryption hierarchy, assuming that we have the DMK created in the previous steps:

```
1> ALTER MASTER KEY REGENERATE
2> WITH ENCRYPTION BY PASSWORD = 'S0m3C001p4sw00rdforN3wK3y'
3> GO
```

Opening the DMK for use:

```
1> OPEN MASTER KEY
2> DECRYPTION BY PASSWORD = 'S0m3C001p4sw00rdforN3wK3y'
3> GO
```

 If the DMK was encrypted with the SMK, it will be automatically opened when it is needed for decryption or encryption. In this case, it is not necessary to use the `OPEN MASTER KEY` statement.

Closing the DMK after use:

```
1> CLOSE MASTER KEY
2> GO
```

Backing up the DMK:

```
1> USE Sandbox
2> GO
1> OPEN MASTER KEY
2> DECRYPTION BY PASSWORD = 'S0m3C001p4sw00rdforN3wK3y';
3> BACKUP MASTER KEY TO FILE = '/var/opt/mssql/backup/Snadbox-dmk'
4> ENCRYPTION BY PASSWORD = 'fk58smk@sw0h%as2'
5> GO
```

Restoring the DMK:

```
1> USE Sandbox
2> GO
1> RESTORE MASTER KEY
2> FROM FILE = '/var/opt/mssql/backup/Snadbox-dmk'
3> DECRYPTION BY PASSWORD = 'fk58smk@sw0h%as2'
4> ENCRYPTION BY PASSWORD = 'S0m3C001p4sw00rdforN3wK3y';
5> GO
```

When the master key is restored, SQL Server decrypts all the keys that are encrypted with the currently active master key, and then encrypts these keys with the restored master.

Dropping the DMK:

```
1> USE Sandbox
2> GO
1> DROP MASTER KEY
2> GO
```

Transparent Data Encryption

SQL Server has two ways of encrypting data. One way is by protecting data at rest, and the second is by protecting it in transit.

Imagine the following scenario: someone has unauthorized access to your database system environment. That person finds a way to get the last database backup file, copies it, and takes it to an unsecured environment. At this moment, the security mechanism just fell apart.

This scenario illustrates what can happen when someone illegally copies, detaches, and restores your database. The consequences of such activity can be substantial, depending on the sensitivity of your data environment.

Those unpleasant situations can be avoided by using **Transparent Data Encryption** (TDE).

TDE performs real-time I/O encryption and decryption of the data and log files. The encryption uses a **database encryption key** (DEK) which is secured by using a certificate stored in the master database of the server or an asymmetric key. It provides the ability to comply with many laws, regulations, and guidelines established in various industries. This enables software developers to encrypt data by using AES encryption algorithms without changing existing applications.

TDE does not provide client/server encryption, but system database `tempdb` will be encrypted.

Backup files of databases that have TDE enabled are also encrypted by using the DEK. As a result, when you restore these backup files, the certificate protecting the DEK must be available. This means that, in addition to backing up the database, you have to make sure that you maintain backups of the server certificates to prevent data loss. Data loss will result if the certificate is no longer available:

To implement TDE, we need to follow these steps:

1. Create a master key in the master database.
2. Create a certificate protected by using the master key.
3. Create a database encryption key and protect it by using the certificate.
4. Create a database encryption key and protect it by using the certificate.
5. Set the database to use encryption.

```
1> USE master;
2> GO
1> CREATE MASTER KEY ENCRYPTION
2> BY PASSWORD = 'Some3xtr4Passw00rd';
3> GO
1> SELECT name, create_date
2> FROM sys.symmetric_keys
3> GO
name                         create_date
-------------------------    ------------------------
##MS_DatabaseMasterKey##     2017-05-14 12:02:59.630
##MS_ServiceMasterKey##      2017-04-17 17:56:20.793
(2 row(s) affected)
1> CREATE CERTIFICATE TDE
2> WITH SUBJECT = 'TDE-Certificate';
3> GO
1> SELECT name, expiry_date
2> FROM sys.certificates
3> WHERE name = 'TDE'
4> GO
name                         expiry_date
-------------------------    ------------------------
TDE                          2018-05-14 10:03:44.000
(1 row(s) affected)
1> USE Sandbox
2> GO
```

```
1> CREATE DATABASE ENCRYPTION KEY
2> WITH ALGORITHM = AES_256
3> ENCRYPTION BY SERVER CERTIFICATE TDE
4> GO
Warning: The certificate used for encrypting the database
encryption key has not been backed up.
1> ALTER DATABASE Sandbox
2> SET ENCRYPTION ON
3> GO
```

 You are done. TDE is now in the operation mode. To test it, you will need to detach this database, and drop the certificate and master key. After that try to attach the database again. You should get an error message.

Backup encryption

This feature is very close to TDE, but there is a difference: TDE is a transparent process. Data is encrypted on-the-fly into the database, and decrypted on the way out. But what if we don't want to encrypt the whole database? Encryption is a CPU time-consuming task. Data needs to be encrypted and decrypted all the time. With a large number of user requests, this can be an issue if we don't scale our hardware to follow this security feature.

In some business scenarios, we need only to worry about backup file security. TDE handle this part as well, but we need to turn on TDE. Backup encryption solves this problem in the way that SQL Server only encrypts backup files after the backup procedure. So, if anyone gets their hands on backup files, without corresponding keys it will be useless.

In the following steps, we'll create a backup certificate, create a backup file of our `Sandbox` database, and do compression and encryption with the certificate:

```
1> USE master;
2> GO

1> CREATE CERTIFICATE BackupCert
2> WITH SUBJECT = 'Database encrypted backups';
3> GO

1> BACKUP DATABASE Sandbox
2> TO DISK = '/var/opt/mssql/backup/Sandbox.bak'
3> WITH
4> COMPRESSION,
5> ENCRYPTION
6> (
```

```
7> ALGORITHM = AES_256,
8> SERVER CERTIFICATE = BackupCert
9> ),
10> STATS = 10
11> GO
```

 Warning: The certificate used for encrypting the database encryption key has not been backed up. You should immediately back up the certificate and the private key associated with the certificate. If the certificate ever becomes unavailable or if you need to restore or attach the database on another server, you must have backups of both the certificate and the private key or you will not be able to open the database.

Symmetric encryption

Symmetric encryption is the type of encryption that uses the same key for encryption and decryption. SQL Server allows you to choose from several algorithms, including DES, Triple DES, TRIPLE_DES_3KEY, RC2, RC4, 128-bit RC4, DESX, 128-bit AES, 192-bit AES, and 256-bit AES.

No single algorithm is ideal for all situations. However, the following general principles apply:

- Strong encryption requires more CPU resources
- Long keys generally yield stronger encryption than short keys
- Asymmetric encryption is stronger than symmetric encryption if using the same key size; but performance is compromised
- Long and strong passwords are better than short and/or weak passwords
- If you are encrypting large amounts of data, you should encrypt using a symmetric key because of performance issues
- Encrypted data cannot be compressed, but compressed data can be encrypted

When a symmetric key is created, it must be encrypted by using at least one of the following:

- Certificate
- Password
- Symmetric key
- Asymmetric key

The key can have more than one encryption of each type. In other words, a single symmetric key can be encrypted by using multiple certificates, passwords, symmetric keys, and asymmetric keys at the same time.

In the following lines, you will see how symmetric encryption works. Here is our scenario:

- In the database `Sandbox`, you will create the table `EncryptedCustomer`
- We will import all records from the `AdventureWorks.Person.Person` table
- During import, we will trigger the encryption process of sensitive data
- The imported record will be in AES 256 format

Let's start:

```
1> USE Sandbox
2> GO

1> CREATE MASTER KEY
2> ENCRYPTION BY PASSWORD = 'Some3xtr4Passw00rd';
3> GO

-- Create new table for encryption process
1> CREATE TABLE EncryptedCustomer(
3> CustomerID int NOT NULL PRIMARY KEY,
4> FirstName varbinary(200),
5> MiddleName varbinary(200),
6> LastName varbinary(200),
7> EmailAddress varbinary(200),
8> Phone varbinary(150));
9> GO
-- Create a certificate
1> CREATE CERTIFICATE Cert4SymKey
2> ENCRYPTION BY PASSWORD = 'pGFD4bb925DGvbd2439587y'
3> WITH SUBJECT = 'Protection of symmetric key',
4> EXPIRY_DATE = '20201031';
5> GO

-- Create a AES 256 symmetric key
1> CREATE SYMMETRIC KEY CustomerSymKey
2> WITH ALGORITHM = AES_256,
3> IDENTITY_VALUE = 'NTK2016'
4> ENCRYPTION BY CERTIFICATE Cert4SymKey;
5> GO

-- Open the key that's protected by certificate
1> OPEN SYMMETRIC KEY CustomerSymKey
2> DECRYPTION BY CERTIFICATE Cert4SymKey
3> WITH PASSWORD = 'pGFD4bb925DGvbd2439587y';
```

```
4> GO

-- Encrypt the data
1> INSERT INTO EncryptedCustomer(
2> CustomerID,
3> FirstName,
4> MiddleName,
5> LastName,
6> EmailAddress,
7> Phone)
8> SELECT
9> P.BusinessEntityID,
10> EncryptByKey(Key_Guid('CustomerSymKey'),FirstName),
11> EncryptByKey(Key_Guid('CustomerSymKey'),MiddleName),
12> EncryptByKey(Key_Guid('CustomerSymKey'),LastName),
13> EncryptByKey(Key_Guid('CustomerSymKey'),EA.EmailAddress),
14> EncryptByKey(Key_Guid('CustomerSymKey'), PP.PhoneNumber)
15> FROM AdventureWorks.Person.Person AS P
16> INNER JOIN AdventureWorks.Person.EmailAddress AS EA
17> ON P.BusinessEntityID = EA.BusinessEntityID
18> INNER JOIN AdventureWorks.Person.PersonPhone AS PP
19> ON P.BusinessEntityID = PP.BusinessEntityID
20> GO

-- Close the key
1> CLOSE SYMMETRIC KEY CustomerSymKey
2> GO

-- View encrypted binary data
1> SELECT FirstName
2> FROM EncryptedCustomer
3> GO

-- Open the key again and decrypt column side by side
1> OPEN SYMMETRIC KEY CustomerSymKey
2> DECRYPTION BY CERTIFICATE Cert4SymKey
3> WITH PASSWORD = 'pGFD4bb925DGvbd2439587y'
4> GO

1> SELECT
2> CAST(DecryptByKey(FirstName) AS nvarchar(100)) AS
3> DecryptedFirstName, FirstName
4> FROM EncryptedCustomer;
5> GO
```

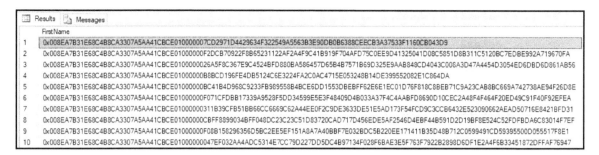

Figure 9-6. Content of column FirstName

Row-level security

This feature is new, starting from version SQL Server 2016. Row-level security was a security challenge for a long time. It was implemented through different sets of add-ons and tools. However, this is now built into the database engine and SQL language. Imagine this scenario: a sales person has read permission on the `Sales` table, but you want each sales person to only see their own sales records, and the manager should see all the records. If you look at this problem through the classic user-permission chain, it is impossible to implement it. However, the row-level security feature makes it possible.

Let's see how it works:

```
1> USE Sandbox
2> GO

--Create three users without logins
1> CREATE USER Manager WITHOUT LOGIN;
2> CREATE USER Sales1 WITHOUT LOGIN;
3> CREATE USER Sales2 WITHOUT LOGIN;
4> GO

-- Create Sales table
1> CREATE TABLE Sales(
2> OrderID int,
3> SalesRep sysname,
4> Product varchar(10),
5> Qty int )
6> GO

-- Add some sample data
1> INSERT Sales VALUES
2> (1, 'Sales1', 'Valve', 5),
```

```
3> (2, 'Sales1', 'Wheel', 2),
4> (3, 'Sales1', 'Valve', 4),
5> (4, 'Sales2', 'Bracket', 2),
6> (5, 'Sales2', 'Wheel', 5),
7> (6, 'Sales2', 'Seat', 5);
8> GO
-- Execute SELECT statement under your permission
1> SELECT * FROM Sales;
2> GO


-- Give to all users necessary read permissions
1> GRANT SELECT ON Sales TO Manager
2> GO
1> GRANT SELECT ON Sales TO Sales1
2> GO
1> GRANT SELECT ON Sales TO Sales2
2> GO


-- Create new schema
1> CREATE SCHEMA Security;
2> GO


--Creating new function which will user SalesRep as input
1> CREATE FUNCTION
2> Security.fn_securitypredicate(@SalesRep AS sysname)
3> RETURNS TABLE
4> WITH SCHEMABINDING
5> AS
6> RETURN SELECT 1 AS fn_securitypredicate_result
7> WHERE @SalesRep = USER_NAME() OR USER_NAME() = 'Manager'
8> GO


--Creating security policy for the data filtering
1> CREATE SECURITY POLICY SalesFilter
2> ADD FILTER PREDICATE
3> Security.fn_securitypredicate(SalesRep)
4> ON dbo.Sales
5> WITH (STATE = ON);
6> GO
--Now execute SELECT in the context of the new users
1> EXECUTE AS USER = 'Sales1'
2> SELECT * FROM Sales
3> REVERT
4> GO


1> EXECUTE AS USER = 'Sales2'
2> SELECT * FROM Sales
3> REVERT
```

```
4> GO

1> EXECUTE AS USER = 'Manager'
2> SELECT * FROM Sales
3> REVERT
4> GO

-- If you need you can turn off this policy
1> ALTER SECURITY POLICY SalesFilter
2> WITH (STATE = OFF);
3> GO
```

 Row-level security does not encrypt any data. It basically just filters content based on the input parameter of the function. This feature can be used in many business scenarios. Some of the examples are ad-hoc querying, reporting, analyzing, exporting, and so on, where users need to have rows filtered on the row level not the column.

Dynamic data masking

Another great security feature is presented in version SQL Server 2016. Dynamic data masking limits sensitive data exposure by masking it to users with low-level privileges. Sometimes you will need to expose some elements from the data, but with built-in elements of preventing unauthorized access. Let's look at the following example: a user will execute SELECT, but unauthorized elements are hidden-masked:

ID	FirstName	LastName	PhoneNumber	EmailAddress	Credit CardNumber
1	Jasmin	Azemović	+387- xxxxxx	jxx@xxxx.com	xxxx-xxxx-xxxx-1111
2	Denis	Musić	+387- xxxxxx	dxx@xxxx.com	xxxx-xxxx-xxxx-2222
3	Edward	Snowden	+387- xxxxxx	exx@xxxx.com	xxxx-xxxx-xxxx-3333
4	Julian	Assange	+387- xxxxxx	jxx@live.com	xxxx-xxxx-xxxx-4444

This feature can be implemented without affecting or modifying any existing SQL or application code.

Let's see how it works:

```
-- You will use content of AdventureWorks sample database
1> USE AdventureWorks
2> GO

-- Add masked future to the Email column
1> ALTER TABLE Person.EmailAddress
2> ALTER COLUMN EmailAddress
3> ADD MASKED WITH (FUNCTION = 'email()')
4> GO

--New user without login and read permission
1> CREATE USER UnauthorizedUser WITHOUT LOGIN
2> GO
3> GRANT SELECT ON Person.EmailAddress TO UnauthorizedUser
4> GO

--Execute SELECT in the contenxrt of UnauthorizedUser
1> EXECUTE AS USER = 'UnauthorizedUser'
2> SELECT TOP 5 EmailAddressID, EmailAddress
3> FROM Person.EmailAddress
4> REVERT
5> GO
EmailAddressID EmailAddress
-------------- ----------------
           798 aXXX@XXXX.com
          1516 aXXX@XXXX.com
           509 aXXX@XXXX.com
          1467 aXXX@XXXX.com
          4690 aXXX@XXXX.com

(5 row(s) affected)

--Execute SELECT in the context of the sa user
1> SELECT TOP 5 EmailAddressID, EmailAddress
2> FROM Person.EmailAddress
3> GO

EmailAddressID EmailAddress
-------------- ------------------------------
798            a0@adventure-works.com
1516           a1@adventure-works.com
509            aaron0@adventure-works.com
1467           aaron1@adventure-works.com
4690           aaron10@adventure-works.com

(5 row(s) affected)
```

Dynamic data masking does not prevent database users from connecting directly to the database and running ad-hoc queries that can expose sensitive data. It is highly recommended to use this feature in combination with other security features for better protection.

Summary

Protecting data is the most important thing in database environments. When all security elements fail (for instance, installation errors, authentication, authorization, bad access policy, and so on), there is no more protection. This chapter looked at how to implement advanced techniques for protecting data, such as cryptography and advanced built-in SQL Server on Linux security features.

In the next chapter, we will introduce the basic elements of SQL Server indexing.

10
Indexing

In the database world, faster means better. Every query, no matter how well written, can execute faster. If we look from a different angle, every query over time can execute slower than it initially did. Everything is okay with your database, but the internal mechanisms of inserting, updating, and deleting can create fragmentation inside database files, which can cause a degradation in performance. There are many reasons for poor performance: one of them is the inappropriate process of indexing data inside the tables. SQL Server has strong indexing foundations.

This chapter will introduce you to the basics of:

- Indexing concepts
- Clustered index
- Concept of heap
- Non-clustered index
- Columnstore index

Indexing concepts

Imagine a small book of 100 pages. Let's say that this hypothetical book is about the SQL language. Your only navigation through the book is via the **Table of Contents** (**TOC**) with page numbers. Now, imagine that you need to find where the word DDL is mentioned in the book. The TOC is useless. You can find a chapter about DDL commands, if it exists, but there is no guarantee that DDL is not mentioned anywhere else. You have to conclude that the only way to find all DDL words is by reading all 100 pages, page by page.

Now, let's imagine the same book with an Index of Terms. It means you will have all the book's related words in some order (for example, ascending) with the number of the page(s) where that word is positioned in the book. In our example, let's say that DDL is mentioned on pages 33, 56, and 78 of the book. Now there is no need to read each page; you can look at the index and quickly locate the required data.

The same concept is applied in the database world. Tables with the data can be indexed to ensure that your query locates data more efficiently. An index is a collection of the column data associated with a table. Indexes can be used to improve the performance of queries or enforce data uniqueness. However, the primary use is to point to the location of the requested data and to minimize the need for scanning the entire table.

Accessing the data

SQL Server accesses data in one of two ways:

By scanning all the data pages in a table (table scan). When SQL Server performs a table scan, it:

- Starts at the beginning of the table
- Scans from page to page through all the rows in the table
- Extracts the rows that satisfied the criteria of the query

When SQL Server uses an index, it:

- Goes through the index tree structure to find rows that the query requests
- Extracts only the rows that satisfy search criteria

Whenever SQL Server needs to access data in a table, it needs to makes a decision about whether to read all the pages of the table or whether there are one or more indexes on the table that would reduce the amount of read operations.

Indexes are not described in ANSI SQL standards. The database itself can function without it, but accessing data by reading large numbers of pages is usually considerably slower than methods that use appropriate indexes. Indexes are considered to be part of the implementation.

Index structure

Indexes in database systems are often based on tree (B-tree) structures. **Binary trees (B-trees)** are simple structures where, at each level, a decision is made to navigate left or right. This style of tree can become unbalanced and less useful.

On the other hand, SQL Server on Linux indexes are based on self-balancing trees, where binary trees have at most two children per node. Also, SQL Server indexes can have a large number of children per node. This improves the efficiency of the indexes and avoids the need for frequent depth scans within an index.

For operations that read data, indexes perform best when each page of the index is full. While indexes may initially start full, modifications to the data in the indexes can cause the need to split index pages. Modification can occur when users modify data inside the table.

For example, the original record was on page 45, but after modification it has now spanned across two pages, 45 and 46. This information needs to be updated in the index structure. The conclusion is that frequent data changes are not index-friendly. Because of this side effect, it is important to choose only the required columns for the indexing procedure.

Single and composite indexes

Indexes in general are based on data from single columns. Indexes can also be based on the data from multiple columns. In business applications, composite indexes are often more useful than single-column indexes. The key advantage of composite indexes is higher selectivity.

An example could be searching for students and details about their grades. This is an example of a composite index. In the absence of any other criteria, when designing composite indexes you should index the most selective column first.

Ascending and descending indexes

Each index can be created in ascending or descending order. For single-column indexes, ascending and descending indexes are equally efficient. For composite indexes, specifying the order of individual columns within the index might be useful. For example, you might need to output grades by date descending, with students ascending. In this case scenario, you will get the grades with recent dates faster.

Further detail on this is beyond the scope of this book. The information provided should be enough to understand the basic concept and start to implement concrete index types.

Clustered index

A clustered index sorts and stores the data rows of the table in an order based on the clustered index key. The clustered index is implemented as a B-tree where every page in a tree is called an index node. Because a clustered index determines the order in which table rows are actually stored, each table can have only one clustered index, and the table's rows cannot be stored in more than one order.

Because you can have only one clustered index per table, you must ensure that you use it to achieve the maximum benefits. Before you create a clustered index, you need to understand how your data will be accessed.

Clustered indexes are most effective when used to support queries that do the following:

- Return a range of values by using operators such as BETWEEN, >, >=, <, and <=
- Return data sorted using the ORDER BY or GROUP BY clause
- Return data combined by using JOIN clauses; typically these are foreign key columns
- Return large result sets

When you define a PRIMARY KEY on a user table, SQL Server will automatically create a clustered index on that column. In most business scenarios, that will be the int data type with the IDENTITY option.

Here are some examples of how you can create a clustered index through SQL code:

```
1> USE Sandbox
2> GO

-- This example will automatically create clustered index on PatientID
column
1> CREATE TABLE Patients (
2> PatientID int IDENTITY (1,1) PRIMARY KEY,
3> LastName nvarchar (15) NOT NULL,
4> FirstName nvarchar (15) NOT NULL,
5> Email nvarchar (15) NOT NULL)
```

```
5> GO

-- You can add clustered index after you create the table
1> CREATE TABLE Telemetry (
2> TelemetryID int IDENTITY (1,1),
3> TelemetryData xml NOT NULL)
4> GO

1> CREATE CLUSTERED INDEX CL_TelemetryID
2> ON Telemetry (TelemetryID)

--You can check indexes with this system catalog view
1> SELECT name FROM sys.indexes
2> WHERE type = 1 --clustered index
3> ORDER BY object_id DESC
4> GO

name
---------------------------------
queue_clustered_index
queue_clustered_index
queue_clustered_index
CL_TelemetryID
PK__Patients__970EC346FB2AFC49
wpr_bucket_clustered_idx
```

Your output can be different but you should find indexes from previous examples. In my case, CL_TelemetryID is easy to spot. The first example from the Patients table has a generic name, PK__Patients__970EC346FB2AFC49.

 One important thing to note is that a clustered index does not always need to be PK. In some scenarios, you will choose some other column.

What is a heap

Imagine a library where every book is just placed in any available space. To find a particular book, you need to scan through all the bookshelves. From the database perspective, there is a structure with the same properties called a **heap**. A heap is the simplest table structure available in SQL Server.

A heap is a table without a clustered index. The data rows are not stored in any specific order, and there is no specific order to quickly find a particular data page. Data rows are added to the first available location within the table's pages that have sufficient space. If no space is available, additional pages are added to the table and the rows placed in those pages.

Consider using a heap for tables that:

- **Contain volatile data where rows are added, deleted, and updated frequently**: The overhead of index maintenance can be costlier than the benefits
- **Contain small amounts of data**: Using a table scan to find data can be quicker than maintaining and using an index
- **Contain data that is written and rarely read, such as an audit log**: An index can be an unnecessary storage and maintenance overhead

Here is a SQL query to check if there are any heap structures inside a database where this query is executed:

```
1> SELECT O.name, O.object_id
2> FROM sys.objects O
3> INNER JOIN sys.partitions P
4> ON P.object_id = O.object_id
5> WHERE P.index_id =0
6> GO
```

 The conclusion is that heaps are not such good structures from the point of view of performance. If you need to write any query on a particular table, a heap is not an option. You should avoid them where possible. Unfortunately, in real-life scenarios you will find many examples of tables in heap structures. Over time, these objects become performance bottlenecks.

Non-clustered index

You can freely call these a user index. In most case scenarios, non-clustered indexes are created based on search criteria and business requirements. For example, users of your application will search based on `LastName` and `ProductName`. These attributes are not primary keys (in this universe), but you need to use the power of indexing techniques. From the SQL Server perspective, non-clustered indexes are the right choice.

Non-clustered indexes have almost the same structure as clustered indexes. The only difference is that the data rows in the tables are not sorted based on their non-clustered keys. In the non-clustered index, the data and the index are stored separately.

Non-clustered indexes are designed to improve the performance of frequently used queries that are not covered by a clustered index. If your table already has a clustered index and you need to index another column, you have no choice but to use a non-clustered index. You can achieve maximum query performance improvements when an index contains all columns from a query. This is the reason why you need to make plans for your indexing strategy. However, too many indexes can result in side effects.

Consider using a non-clustered index when:

- You want to improve the performance of queries that use JOIN or GROUP BY clauses
- Your table has a low update frequency but contains large volumes of data
- You know that your queries do not return large result sets
- You need to index columns that are frequently used in the search conditions of a query, such as a WHERE clause, that returns exact matches
- You need to index columns that contain many distinct values, such as a combination of last name and first name

Now let's play a little bit with non-clustered indexes. You will learn how to create them, include new columns, change the definition of an index, delete, and reorganize the content of an index the content of an index with the following code:

```
1> USE Sandbox
2> GO

1> CREATE TABLE Books (
2> BookID nvarchar(20) PRIMARY KEY,
3> PublisherID int NOT NULL,
4> Title nvarchar(50) NOT NULL,
5> ReleaseDate date NOT NULL)
6> GO

--Create nonclusterd composite index on two columns
1> CREATE NONCLUSTERED INDEX IX_Book_Publisher
2> ON Books (PublisherID, ReleaseDate DESC);
3> GO

--Disabling of an index.
1> ALTER INDEX IX_Book_Publisher
2> ON Books
```

```
3> DISABLE
4> GO

--Dropping of an index
1> DROP INDEX IX_Book_Publisher
2> ON Books
3> GO

--Creating same index but with included column Title
1> CREATE NONCLUSTERED INDEX IX_Book_Publisher
2> ON Books (PublisherID, ReleaseDate DESC)
3> INCLUDE (Title);
4> GO

--Process of reorganizing an index if fragmentation is low
1> ALTER INDEX IX_Book_Publisher
2> ON Books
3> REORGANIZE
4> GO

----Process of rebuilding an index if fragmentation is high
1> ALTER INDEX IX_Book_Publisher
2> ON Books
3> REBUILD
```

Unique indexes

Special types of indexes are unique indexes. Sometimes you will need to maintain uniqueness on an attribute that is not a good candidate for the primary key, for example, Email or LoginName. A unique index will ensure that there are no duplicate values inside the table in that specific column.

 NULL if stored one time is still considered unique.

Here is an example on the Patients table:

```
1> CREATE UNIQUE NONCLUSTERED INDEX UQ_Patient_Email
2> ON Patients (Email ASC)
3> GO
```

Columnstore index

From version SQL Server 2012, the database engine includes new types of indexes called columnstore indexes, which are in-memory structures that use compression technology to organize index data in a column-based format instead of the row-based format that traditional indexes use. Columnstore indexes are specifically designed to improve the performance of queries against data warehouse environments where you need to deal with large fact tables and related dimension tables. There are two types of columnstore indexes:

A non-clustered columnstore index is a read-only index that you can create on a table that has an existing standard clustered index, or on a table that is a heap. Like a standard non-clustered index, a non-clustered columnstore index can include one or more columns from the table.

A clustered columnstore index represents the actual data rows in the table, and is not a separate structure. This means that all columns are included in the index. Unlike non-clustered columnstore indexes, clustered columnstore indexes to do not make the table read-only, so you can update without restrictions.

 An important thing to remember when using clustered columnstore indexes is that when you create one on a specific table, it must be the only index on that object. You cannot use a clustered columnstore index in combination with any other index.

Here is one example on the `AdventureWorks` sample database, in the `SalesOrderDetails` table. From the sample database perspective, it is a large table, with more than 100,000 records. However, in a real-life scenario, it is not a big deal. Improvements based on this type of index make sense on millions of rows. But in any case we will try to *feel* a difference even on small amount of data:

```
1> USE AdventureWorks
2> GO

--Check number of rows
1> SELECT COUNT (*)
2> FROM Sales.SalesOrderDetail
3> GO

-----------
121317

(1 row(s) affected)

1> SELECT TOP 5 ProductID, SUM(UnitPrice) TotalPrice,
```

```
2> AVG(UnitPrice) AvgPrice,
3> SUM(OrderQty) SumOrderQty, AVG(OrderQty) AvgOrderQty
4> FROM Sales.SalesOrderDetail
5> GROUP BY ProductID
6> ORDER BY ProductID
7> GO
```

ProductID	TotalPrice	AvgPrice	SumOrder	AvgOrder
707	95223,1798	30,8865	6266	2
708	91561,731	30,4495	6532	2
709	1063,335	5,656	1107	5
710	250,80	5,70	90	2
711	93827,8566	30,365	6743	2

```
(5 row(s) affected)
```

 Now look at the following screenshot. It was taken on the SQL Server Management Tool in Windows, because there is no GUI tool with this capability yet.

Figure 10-1. Execution plan of the query

```
--Create Nonclustered columnstore on three columns
1> CREATE NONCLUSTERED COLUMNSTORE INDEX
2> IX_SalesOrderDetail_ColumnStore
3> ON Sales.SalesOrderDetail
4> (UnitPrice, OrderQty, ProductID)
5> GO
```

Let's execute the same query again.

You probably didn't notice any significant difference in execution time, but internally there is a huge difference. Take a look at the following screenshot:

Figure 10-2. Execution plan of the query but with columnstore index

The difference is in initial operator type (those diagrams are read from right to left). In the first case, the operator is `Clustered Index Scan` and it took 64% of all query execution time. The second-time operator is `Columnstore Index Scan` and took 19% of query execution time, which is much less than the first time. In your case, the number could be different, but it should be within these boundaries.

Summary

In this chapter, you learned the basic foundations of SQL Server on Linux indexes. You should now also understand why they are so important for performance, and how to use them in particular business scenarios.

In the next chapter, you will learn about a more advanced topic, that is, addressing performance issues.

11
In-Memory OLTP

In the previous chapter, you learned how index in general can help your queries run faster. But indexing has its limitations. When your I/O subsystem is not performing well in combination with less RAM, then indexing is just a first aid. All these problems will return later with much higher intensity.

Simply adding more RAM, faster disks, and better CPU will solve your problems temporarily. The system will *breathe* better, but you must ask yourself is this it or can I push the limits sky high? Yes, you can. It is amazing what SQL Server can offer you in terms of achieving better performance.

In this chapter, you will get the basics on how to implement In-Memory OLTP on SQL Server on Linux through the following topics:

- Elements of performance
- What is In-Memory OLTP
- Implementation

Elements of performance

How do you know if you have a performance issue in your database environment? Well, let's put it in these terms. You notice it (the good), users start calling technical support and complaining about how everything is slow (the bad) or you don't know about your performance issues (the ugly). Try to never get in to the last category.

The good

Achieving best performance is an iterative process where you need to define a set of tasks that you will execute on a regular basics and monitor their results. Here is a list that will give you an idea and guide you through this process:

- Establish the baseline
- Define the problem
- Fix one thing at a time
- Test and re-establish the baseline
- Repeat everything

Establishing the baseline is the critical part. In most case scenarios, it is not possible without real stress testing. Example: How many users' systems can you handle on the current configuration? The next step is to measure the processing time. Do your queries or stored procedures require milliseconds, seconds, or minutes to execute?

Now you need to monitor your database server using a set of tools and correct methodologies. During that process, you notice that some queries show elements of performance degradation. This is the point that defines the problem.

Let's say that frequent UPDATE and DELETE operations are resulting in index fragmentation. The next step is to fix this issue with REORGANIZE or REBUILD index operations.

Test your solution in the control environment and then in the production. Results can be better, same, or worse. It depends and there is no magic answer here. Maybe now something else is creating the problem: disk, memory, CPU, network, and so on. In this step, you should re-establish the old or a new baseline.

Measuring performance process is something that never ends. You should keep monitoring the system and stay alert.

The bad

If you are in this category, then you probably have an issue with establishing the baseline and alerting the system. So, users are becoming your alerts and that is a bad thing. The rest of the steps are the same except re-establishing the baseline. But this can be your wake-up call to move yourself in the *good* category.

The ugly

This means that you don't know or you don't want to know about performance issues. The best case scenario is a headline on some news portal, but that is the *ugly* thing. Every decent DBA should try to be light years away from this category.

What do you need to start working with performance measuring, monitoring, and fixing?

Here are some tips that can help you:

- Know the data and the app
- Know your server and its capacity
- Use dynamic management views—DMVs:
    - sys.dm_os_wait_stats
    - sys.dm_exec_query_stats
    - sys.dm_db_index_operational_stats
- Look for top queries by reads, writes, CPU, execution count
- Put everything in to LibreOffice Calc or another spreadsheet application and do some basic comparative math

Fortunately, there is something in the field that can make your life really easy. It can boost your environment to the scale of warp speed (I am a *Star Trek* fan).

What is In-Memory OLTP?

SQL Server In-Memory feature is unique in the database world. The reason is very simple; because it is built-in to the databases' engine itself. It is not a separate database solution and there are some major benefits of this. One of these benefits is that in most cases you don't have to rewrite entire SQL Server applications to see performance benefits. On average, you will see 10x more speed while you are testing the new In-Memory capabilities. Sometimes you will even see up to 50x improvement, but it all depends on the amount of business logic that is done in the database via stored procedures. The greater the logic in the database, the greater the performance increase. The more the business logic sits in the app, the less opportunity there is for performance increase. This is one of the reasons for always separating database world from the rest of the application layer.

It has built-in compatibility with other non-memory tables. This way you can optimize the memory you have for the most heavily used tables and leave others on the disk. This also means you won't have to go out and buy expensive new hardware to make large In-Memory databases work; you can optimize In-Memory to fit your existing hardware.

In-Memory was started in SQL Server 2014. One of the first companies that has started to use this feature during the development of the 2014 version was Bwin. This is an online gaming company. With In-Memory OLTP they improved their transaction speed by 16x, without investing in new expensive hardware.

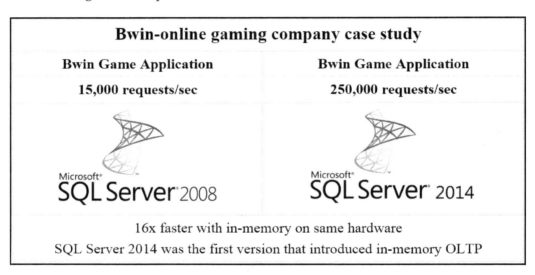

Table 11-1. BWIN In-memory OLTP Case study

 The same company has achieved **1.2 Million requests/second** on SQL Server 2016 with a single machine using In-Memory OLTP:
https://blogs.msdn.microsoft.com/sqlcat/2016/10/26/how-bwin-is-u
sing-sql-server-2016-in-memory-oltp-to-achieve-unprecedented-
performance-and-scale/

Not every application will benefit from In-Memory OLTP. If an application is not suffering from performance problems related to concurrency, IO pressure, or blocking, it's probably not a good candidate. If the application has long-running transactions that consume large amounts of buffer space, such as ETL processing, it's probably not a good candidate either.

The best applications for consideration would be those that run high volumes of small fast transactions, with repeatable query plans such as order processing, reservation systems, stock trading, and ticket processing. The biggest benefits will be seen on systems that suffer performance penalties from tables that are having concurrency issues related to a large number of users and locking/blocking. Applications that heavily use the `tempdb` for temporary tables could benefit from In-Memory OLTP by creating the table as memory optimized, and performing the expensive sorts, and groups, and selective queries on the tables that are memory optimized.

In-Memory OLTP quick start

An important thing to remember is that the databases that will contain memory-optimized tables must have a MEMORY_OPTIMIZED_DATA filegroup. This filegroup is used for storing the checkpoint needed by SQL Server to recover the memory-optimized tables.

Here is a simple DDL SQL statement to create a database that is prepared for In-Memory tables:

```
1> USE master
2> GO

1> CREATE DATABASE InMemorySandbox
2> ON
3> PRIMARY (NAME = InMemorySandbox_data,
4> FILENAME =
5> '/var/opt/mssql/data/InMemorySandbox_data_data.mdf',
6> size=500MB),
7> FILEGROUP InMemorySandbox_fg
8> CONTAINS MEMORY_OPTIMIZED_DATA
9> (NAME = InMemorySandbox_dir,
10> FILENAME =
11> '/var/opt/mssql/data/InMemorySandbox_dir')
12> LOG ON (name = InMemorySandbox_log,
13> Filename=
14>'/var/opt/mssql/data/InMemorySandbox_data_data.ldf',
15> size=500MB)
16 GO
```

The next step is to alter the existing database and configure it to access memory-optimized tables. This part is helpful when you need to test and/or migrate current business solutions:

```
--First, we need to check compatibility level of database.
-- Minimum is 130
1> USE AdventureWorks
2> GO
3> SELECT T.compatibility_level
4> FROM sys.databases as T
5> WHERE T.name = Db_Name();
6> GO

compatibility_level
-------------------
120

(1 row(s) affected)

--Change the compatibility level
1> ALTER DATABASE CURRENT
2> SET COMPATIBILITY_LEVEL = 130;
3> GO

--Modify the transaction isolation level
1> ALTER DATABASE CURRENT SET
2> MEMORY_OPTIMIZED_ELEVATE_TO_SNAPSHOT=ON
3> GO

--Finlay create memory optimized filegroup
1> ALTER DATABASE AdventureWorks
2> ADD FILEGROUP AdventureWorks_fg CONTAINS
3> MEMORY_OPTIMIZED_DATA
4> GO

1> ALTER DATABASE AdventureWorks ADD FILE
2> (NAME='AdventureWorks_mem',
3> FILENAME='/var/opt/mssql/data/AdventureWorks_mem')
4> TO FILEGROUP AdventureWorks_fg
5> GO
```

How to create memory-optimized tables?

The syntax for creating memory-optimized tables is almost the same as the syntax for creating classic disk-based tables. You will need to specify that the table is a memory-optimized table, which is done using the MEMORY_OPTIMIZED = ON clause.

A memory-optimized table can be created with two DURABILITY values:

- SCHEMA_AND_DATA (default)
- SCHEMA_ONLY

If you defined a memory-optimized table with DURABILITY=SCHEMA_ONLY, it means that changes to the table's data are not logged and the data is not persisted on disk. However, the schema is persisted as part of the database metadata. A side effect is that an empty table will be available after the database is recovered during a restart of SQL Server on Linux service.

The following table is a summary of key differences between those two DURABILITY options.

When you create a memory-optimized table, the database engine will generate DML routines just for accessing that table, and load them as DLLs files. SQL Server itself does not perform data manipulation, instead it calls the appropriate DLL:

Conditions	SCHEMA_AND_DATA	SCHEMA_ONLY
Schema is durable	YES	YES
Rows are durable	YES	NO
Is in checkpoint files	YES	NO
Is logged	YES	NO
Is in backup	YES	NO
Speed	Fast	Faster

Table 11-2. Durability differences

Now let's add some memory-optimized tables to our sample database:

```
1> USE InMemorySandbox
2> GO

-- Create a durable memory-optimized table
1> CREATE TABLE Basket(
2> BasketID INT IDENTITY(1,1)
3> PRIMARY KEY NONCLUSTERED,
4> UserID INT NOT NULL INDEX ix_UserID
5> NONCLUSTERED HASH WITH (BUCKET_COUNT=1000000),
6> CreatedDate DATETIME2 NOT NULL,
```

```
7> TotalPrice MONEY) WITH (MEMORY_OPTIMIZED=ON)
8> GO

-- Create a non-durable table.
1> CREATE TABLE UserLogs (
2> SessionID INT IDENTITY(1,1)
3> PRIMARY KEY NONCLUSTERED HASH WITH (BUCKET_COUNT=400000),
4> UserID int NOT NULL,
5> CreatedDate DATETIME2 NOT NULL,
6> BasketID INT,
7> INDEX ix_UserID
8> NONCLUSTERED HASH (UserID) WITH (BUCKET_COUNT=400000))
9> WITH (MEMORY_OPTIMIZED=ON, DURABILITY=SCHEMA_ONLY)
10> GO

-- Add some sample records
1> INSERT INTO UserLogs VALUES
2> (432, SYSDATETIME(), 1),
3> (231, SYSDATETIME(), 7),
4> (256, SYSDATETIME(), 7),
5> (134, SYSDATETIME(), NULL),
6> (858, SYSDATETIME(), 2),
7> (965, SYSDATETIME(), NULL)
8> GO

1> INSERT INTO Basket VALUES
2> (231, SYSDATETIME(), 536),
3> (256, SYSDATETIME(), 6547),
4> (432, SYSDATETIME(), 23.6),
5> (134, SYSDATETIME(), NULL)
6> GO

-- Checking the content of the tables
1> SELECT SessionID, UserID, BasketID
2> FROM UserLogs
3> GO
```

SessionID	UserID	BasketID
1	432	1
2	231	7
3	256	7
4	134	NULL
5	858	2
6	965	NULL

```
(6 row(s) affected)
```

```
1> SELECT BasketID, UserID
2> FROM Basket
3> GO

BasketID        UserID
-------------   -----------
1               231
2               256
3               432
4               134

(4 row(s) affected)
```

What is natively compiled stored procedure?

This is another great feature that comes comes within In-Memory package. In a nutshell, it is a classic SQL stored procedure, but it is compiled into machine code for blazing fast performance. They are stored as native DLLs, enabling faster data access and more efficient query execution than traditional T-SQL.

Now you will create a natively compiled stored procedure to insert 1,000,000 rows into `Basket`:

```
1> USE InMemorySandbox
2> GO

1> CREATE PROCEDURE dbo.usp_BasketInsert @InsertCount int
2> WITH NATIVE_COMPILATION, SCHEMABINDING AS
3> BEGIN ATOMIC
4> WITH
5> (TRANSACTION ISOLATION LEVEL = SNAPSHOT,
6> LANGUAGE = N'us_english')
7> DECLARE @i int = 0
8> WHILE @i < @InsertCount
9> BEGIN
10> INSERT INTO dbo.Basket VALUES (1, SYSDATETIME() , NULL)
11> SET @i += 1
12> END
13> END
14> GO
--Add 1000000 records
1> EXEC dbo.usp_BasketInsert 1000000
2> GO
```

The insert part should be blazing fast. Again, it depends on your environment (CPU, RAM, disk, and virtualization). My insert was done in less than three seconds, on an average machine. But significant improvement should be visible now. Execute the following SELECT statement and count the number of records:

```
1> SELECT COUNT(*)
2> FROM dbo.Basket
3> GO


-----------
1000004

(1 row(s) affected)
```

In my case, counting of one million records was less than one second. It is really hard to achieve this performance on any kind of disk.

Let's try another query. We want to know how much time it will take to find the top 10 records where the insert time was longer than 10 microseconds:

```
1> SELECT TOP 10 BasketID, CreatedDate
2> FROM dbo.Basket
3> WHERE DATEDIFF
4> (MICROSECOND, '2017-05-30 15:17:20.9308732', CreatedDate)
5> >10
6> GO

BasketID          CreatedDate
---------------   ----------------------------
999542            2017-05-30 15:17:20.9349303
999543            2017-05-30 15:17:20.9349303
999544            2017-05-30 15:17:20.9349303
999545            2017-05-30 15:17:20.9349303
999546            2017-05-30 15:17:20.9349303
999547            2017-05-30 15:17:20.9349303
999548            2017-05-30 15:17:20.9349303
999549            2017-05-30 15:17:20.9349303
999550            2017-05-30 15:17:20.9349303
999551            2017-05-30 15:17:20.9349303

(10 row(s) affected)
```

Again, query execution time was less than a second. Even if you remove `TOP` and try to get all the records it will take less than a second (in my case scenario). Advantages of In-Memory tables are more than obvious.

Summary

In this chapter, you learned what an In-Memory OLTP concept is and how to implement it on new and existing databases. Also, you know that a memory-optimized table can be created with two `DURABILITY` values. Finally, you can create In-Memory tables to achieve best possible performance using this exciting feature.

In the next chapter, we will cover some advanced SQL Server topics and beyond.

12
Beyond SQL Server

This chapter will be an exciting ride through the rest of the different features and tools that can be used in the current state of SQL Server development. As I mentioned in the beginning of Chapter 1, *Linux Distributions*, SQL Server on Linux has just started landing on the Linux planet, and you can definitely expect many improvements in the near future.

This book will probably go out before the final release, so keep that in mind as you read. However, the important thing is that this reference will provide you with more than enough information to quickly start with testing, development, and production without having to read books with more than 500 pages.

Here is the list of the closing topics that we will take a look at in this chapter:

- Query store (feature)
- Temporal tables (feature)
- mssql-scripter (tool)
- DBFS tool (tool)
- DBeaver (third-party tool)

Query store

Sometimes, you will notice that perfectly fine queries will show weak performance for no particular reason. One of the reasons for this could be a change of the execution plan. An execution plan is an internal result SQL Server procedure where the engine needs to decide the best possible way to execute your query. Each query has its own plan. During standard database operations, based on internal statistics, those plans can be changed, but the results are not always better in terms of performance. On the contrary, they can be the exact opposite. Before SQL Server 2016, it was not an easy task to investigate these problems.

You were facing the following issues:

- TTD: Long **time to detect** the issue
- TTM: Long **time to mitigate**

The main reason for this is that the fixing query plan that causes regression is a difficult task to perform. The query plan is not designed for performance troubleshooting. Fortunately, we have this great feature. Query store provides you with insight on the query plan choice and performance. It helps with performance troubleshooting by enabling an option to find performance differences caused by changes in query plans.

Query store automatically captures a history of queries, plans, and statistics, and keeps them for later review and analysis. This allows you to observe database usage patterns and understand when query plan changes occur on the server, and lets you force a particular plan for a specific query.

So, let us see how to activate this cool feature with the following steps and use it on your own queries:

1. Query store is not a feature that automatically starts, and you will need to turn it on. You will use the `AdventureWorks` sample database:

```
1> USE AdventureWorks
2> GO
1> ALTER DATABASE AdventureWorks SET QUERY_STORE = ON
2> GO

--If you want to see more detailed information of what is in the --
query store, run this query
1> SELECT T3.query_text_id, T3.query_sql_text,
2> T2.plan_id, T1.*
3> FROM sys.query_store_query AS T1
4> JOIN sys.query_store_plan AS T2
5> ON T2.query_id = T1.query_id
6> JOIN sys.query_store_query_text AS T3
7> ON T1.query_text_id = T3.query_text_id
```

Please consider this query is visually very inappropriate for the sqlcmd interface. The console is not created for this kind of stuff. In this chapter, you have a quick overview of the third-party GUI tool that can be used for this example or any other example from this book or your own practice.

Because you have just activated this feature, you will not see anything spectacular. But if you run the same query a second time, you will see it on the list. Later, you will see how the number of records your database is working on will rise.

This query will give you a handful of insightful information, such as query text, `plan_id`, compile statistics, duration, CPU, memory, and optimization details. Based on this, you can compare which plan is performing better and force SQL Server to use that particular one.

Now you can write some queries on your own and test the query store feature. Also, you can go back to `Chapter 6`, *A Crash Course in Querying*, if you have any doubts about how to write functional queries on sample databases.

Queries that are executed multiple times will result in that SQL Server engine using different plan(s), which will produce different resource utilization. You can easily detect when the query performance regression occurred and select the optimal plan within a period of interest. Then you can force that optimal plan for future query executions. Some of the reasons why a plan might change are: index fragmentation, wrong index statistics, changes in the distribution of the data, and so on.

You should consider purging query store data based on your needs. This can be done through the set of query store parameters that you can configure through the `ALTER DATABASE` statement, which gives you more control over the whole process. Here are some of them:

- `OPERATION_MODE`
- `DATA_FLUSH_INTERVAL_SECONDS`
- `INTERVAL_LENGTH_MINUTES`
- `MAX_STORAGE_SIZE_MB`
- `QUERY_CAPTURE_MODE`
- `SIZE_BASED_CLEANUP_MODE`
- `CLEANUP_POLICY (STALE_QUERY_THRESHOLD_DAYS)`
- `MAX_PLANS_PER_QUERY`

2. Here are a couple of examples with those options:

```
--Maximum storage size is fixed to 150 MB
1> ALTER DATABASE AdventureWorks
2> SET QUERY_STORE( MAX_STORAGE_SIZE_MB = 150)
3> GO
--Maximum size of query store
--and size based clean up mode is set to AUTO
1> ALTER DATABASE AdventureWorks
2> SET QUERY_STORE(
3> MAX_STORAGE_SIZE_MB = 150,
4> SIZE_BASED_CLEANUP_MODE = AUTO,
5> CLEANUP_POLICY = (STALE_QUERY_THRESHOLD_DAYS = 15))
6> GO
--Purge all the data inside the Query Store
1> ALTER DATABASE AdventureWorks SET QUERY_STORE CLEAR
2> GO
```

For queries that are executed more than once, you may notice that SQL Server used different plans, which resulted in different resource utilization. Query store can help you to easily detect when the query performance regressed, and determine the optimal plan. Based on that information, you can force the optimal plan for query execution.

3. For demonstration purposes, you can use this heavy query on the `AdventureWorks` sample database:

```
1> SELECT P.LastName, P.FirstName, EA.EmailAddress,
2> PP.PhoneNumber,
3> CC.CardNumber,P.FirstName+'.'+P.LastName,
4> SUBSTRING (REVERSE (P.LastName),2,4)+
5> SUBSTRING (REVERSE (P.FirstName),2,2)+
6> SUBSTRING (CAST (P.rowguid AS nvarchar (100)),10,6)
7> FROM Person.Person AS P
8> INNER JOIN
9> Person.EmailAddress AS EA
10> ON P.BusinessEntityID = EA.BusinessEntityID
11> INNER JOIN
12> Person.PersonPhone AS PP
13> ON P.BusinessEntityID = PP.BusinessEntityID
14> LEFT JOIN
15> Sales.PersonCreditCard AS PCC
16> ON PP.BusinessEntityID = PCC.BusinessEntityID
17> LEFT JOIN
18> Sales.CreditCard AS CC
19> ON PCC.CreditCardID = CC.CreditCardID
```

Now execute this query a couple of times.

4. After that, run a query to access the content of the query store with this simplified version for the purpose of reducing the number of columns and adjusting the output to the bash console window:

```
1> SELECT T2.plan_id, T1.query_id,
2> LEFT (T3.query_sql_text,15)
3> FROM sys.query_store_query AS T1
4> JOIN sys.query_store_plan AS T2
5> ON T2.query_id = T1.query_id
6> JOIN sys.query_store_query_text AS T3
7> ON T1.query_text_id = T3.query_text_id

plan_id          query_id
------------     ------------     --------------------
1                2               SELECT P1.LastN ...
(1 row(s) affected)
```

In the time it takes to do this, the plan can change and show regression. Examining query store, you will probably notice that the first version of the plan was performing better. This hypothetical scenario is the ideal candidate for the forcing of the plan.

When a plan is forced on a certain query, every time a query comes to execution, it will be executed with the plan that is forced. The following code will force SQL Server to use plan_id 1 for the query:

```
--Forcing plan_id 1 to be used by query_id 2
1> EXEC sp_query_store_force_plan
2> @query_id = 2, @plan_id = 1
3> GO
```

When using sp_query_store_force_plan, you can only use plans that were recorded by query store as plans for that query. In other words, while query store is active, if you want to remove plan forcing for a particular query and rely on the SQL Server query optimizer, you can use sp_query_store_unforce_plan:

```
--Unforcing plan_id 1 to query_id 2
1> EXEC sp_query_store_unforce_plan
2> @query_id = 1, @plan_id =1
3> GO
```

The query store feature is a great tool that can make your life much easier when you are stuck with performance issues, and it's just a matter of time until this happens. Dealing with query store is more user-friendly through the SQL Server Management Tool, so if you have access to this tool, give yourself some time and explore it. Eventually, the new SQL Server cross-platform administration GUI tool, which is in development, is expected to support many SSMS features and bring them to the Linux platform.

Temporal tables

One of the big issues in the database world is how to deal with historical records. The goal is to keep each version of the record from its initial insertion through its other, different versions over time. It sounds simple, but its implementation is not so easy. DBA and developers were using different tools, techniques, and hacks to achieve this goal. Some of them are as follows:

- Triggers
- Audit logs
- Data warehouses
- Custom solutions

Any of them are efficient, but unfortunately, they are not built into the database engine, and in order to be implemented, it requires some things to be reconsidered:

- Learning new tools
- Learning new concepts
- Administration
- Changes in the application layer

Everything listed here costs time and money. This is the main reason why temporal databases exist as a concept. Microsoft is actually implementing this concept into SQL Server 2016 and subsequent versions, and is calling it **temporal tables**.

So what is it? A temporal table is a database object that provides information about stored facts at any point in time. Temporal tables consist of two separate but connected tables—one for the current data and one for the historical part of the data. SQL Server monitors the data changes in the table with the current data based on the previous values that are stored in the historical table. The database engine provides an interface through SQL statements without any application changes. SQL Server documentation uses system-versioning, and you can find it in Microsoft's official documentation.

In a nutshell, implementation is based on two additional `datetime` (`datetime2` and `datatype`) columns that are used to define a time period from-to a particular record that is or was actually in the system. SQL Server used `SysStartTime` (system start time) to mark when the specific record became active and `SysEndTime` (system and time) to specify the date that the record is valid to:

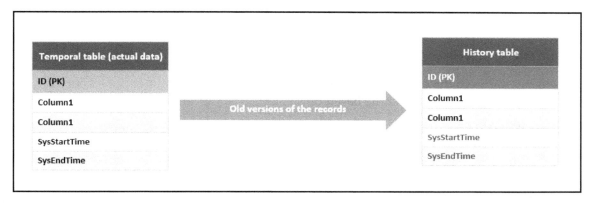

Figure 12-1. How system-versioning works

Now it is time for *query back in time*. The best way to understand how this concept actually works is to write some SQL statements and see it for yourself. For this purpose, I will use an already created `Sandbox` database. You can follow me or you can create a different database:

```
1> USE Sandbox
2> GO

-- Creating pair of system-versioning tables
1> CREATE TABLE Users (
2> UserID int NOT NULL PRIMARY KEY CLUSTERED,
3> LastName varchar(10) NOT NULL,
4> FirstName varchar(10) NOT NULL,
5> Email varchar(20) NULL,
6> SysStartTime datetime2
7> GENERATED ALWAYS AS ROW START NOT NULL,
8> SysEndTime datetime2 GENERATED ALWAYS AS ROW END NOT NULL,
9> PERIOD FOR SYSTEM_TIME (SysStartTime,SysEndTime)
10> )
11> WITH
12> (SYSTEM_VERSIONING = ON
13> (HISTORY_TABLE = dbo.UsersHistory))
14> GO

--Checking the tables trough sys.tabeles, system catalog view
```

```
1> USE Sandbox
2> GO
3> SELECT name, temporal_type_desc
4> FROM sys.tables

name                          temporal_type_desc
----------------------------  ---------------------------------
Users                         SYSTEM_VERSIONED_TEMPORAL_TABLE
UsersHistory                  HISTORY_TABLE

(2 row(s) affected)
```

As you can see from the output, Users is a temporal table and UsersHistory keeps a history of the records through time based on INSERT, UPDATE, and DELETE statements.

I believe that the next example is appropriate to explain what I need to say:

```
-- Adding new record
1> INSERT INTO Users
2> VALUES (1, 'Marty', 'McFly', NULL, DEFAULT, DEFAULT)
3> GO

-- Checking content of the temporal table
1> SELECT UserID, SysStartTime, SysEndTime
2> FROM Users
3> GO

UserID      SysStartTime          SysEndTime
----------  --------------------  --------------------
1           2017-06-12 13:24:34   9999-12-31 23:59:59

(1 row(s) affected)
```

Note that the content of the SysEndTime attribute is 9999-12-31 23:59:59, a default maximum value. It means that this record is valid:

```
--Checking content of history table
1> SELECT *
2> FROM UsersHistory
3> GO

UserID      SysStartTime      SysEndTime
----------  ----------------  ----------------

(0 row(s) affected)
```

```
--Now, we will update Marty's email address
1> UPDATE Users
2> SET Email = 'Marty@HillValley.com'
3> WHERE UserID = 1
4> GO
```

This means that the old record is not valid any more. SQL Server will take the old version (without email) and archive it in the `UsersHistory` table, and then update the record in the `Users` table. Two attributes are about to change: `Email` and `SysStartTime`.

If you want to do any type of time analysis, use the `FOR SYSTEM_TIME` clause, which currently has four temporal subclauses:

- `AS OF`
- `FROM TO`
- `BETWEEN AND`
- `CONTAINED IN`
- `ALL`

You will use the `AS OF` clause when you want to recreate a state of the record at a specific time in the past. On the other hand, `FROM...TO`, `BETWEEN...AND` and `CONTAINED IN` are useful for data audits, and get all changes for a specific record through time.

Let's look at this temporal query, for example:

```
1> SELECT TOP 10 BasketID, CreatedDate
2> FROM dbo.Basket
3> WHERE DATEDIFF (MILLISECOND, '2017-08-09 11:00:20.9308732', CreatedDate)
> 10

UserID      SysStartTime         SysEndTime
----------- -------------------- --------------------
1           2017-06-12 13:24:34  9999-12-31 23:59:59
1           2017-06-12 13:23:00  2017-06-12 13:24:34

(2 row(s) affected)
```

As you can see, the first record shows the current valid record with the new email address. The second record is the past version with a specific time from-until the record was valid.

Sometimes you will need to turn off, or just temporarily disable, system versioning. One good reason for this can be maintenance operations on a temporal table. In any case, you will get two independent tables, one with actual data and one with the history of the data changes. The thing to mention is that there is no data loss in this process.

Let's disable the temporal tables feature on the `Users` table:

```
1> USE Sandbox
2> GO

--Permanently removes SYSTEM_VERSIONING
1> ALTER TABLE Users
2> SET (SYSTEM_VERSIONING = OFF)
3> GO

--Checking the status of tables
1> SELECT name, temporal_type_desc
2> FROM sys.tables
3> GO

name                     temporal_type_desc
----------------------   ------------------------
Users                    NON_TEMPORAL_TABLE
UsersHistory             NON_TEMPORAL_TABLE

(2 row(s) affected)

--Optionally, removes the period columns property
ALTER TABLE Users
DROP PERIOD FOR SYSTEM_TIME
GO
```

Writing temporal queries can be a challenging task, but when you get some practice, you will unlock the huge potential of temporal data and its usage in different business scenarios.

Mssql-scripter tool

Microsoft is pushing really hard to fill in the gaps in the world of Linux regarding SQL Server on Linux. In the Windows environment, it has it all, from the official application over third-party and other commercial, non-commercial, and open source tools.

In this phase of development, CTP 1.3 - RC1, Microsoft started two open source projects on GitHub to help the Linux community become quicker and more productive using SQL Server on Linux. One of them is mssql-scripter (https://github.com/Microsoft/sql-xplat-cli)

It is a cross-platform, command-line interface with the purpose of generating DDL and DML scripts. If you are dealing with databases, then you will appreciate this quite impressive tool. With a simple command, you can export schema from your database, for example, `AdventureWorks`, and recreate it on the other server. Also, it is easy to script all the database data and insert it into a new environment. We can say that mssql-scripter can be used even in the ETL process.

This tool is not a part of standard SQL Server on Linux installation: you will need to install it manually. In the following steps, you will find how to do that. It is built on the top of Python libraries, so you will need a pip. A pip is a tool for managing Python packages.

First, you will need to check the version of pip on your Linux distribution:

```
# pip --version
```

If the version is older than 9.0, or pip is not installed at all, then you should run one of the following commands, depending on your need:

```
# sudo apt-get install python-pip
```

Or:

```
# sudo pip install --upgrade pip
```

After that, you can install the tool using the following command:

```
# sudo pip install mssql-scripter
```

Based on your distro, you may need some additional libraries. If that happens, please refer to https://github.com/Microsoft/sql-xplat-cli.

For the complete list of command options, you can type:

```
# mssql-scripter -h
```

Here, you can find a couple of usage scenarios. As you will see, it is not complicated, and it follows a classic Linux command-line approach.

Export the database schema:

```
# mssql-scripter -S localhost -d AdventureWorks -U sa -f
./AdventureWorks.sql
```

Export the database schema and data:

```
# mssql-scripter -S localhost -d AdventureWorks -U sa --schema-and-data >
./AdventureWorks.sql
```

Script the data to a file:

```
# mssql-scripter -S localhost -d AdventureWorks -U sa --data-only >
./AdventureWorks-data.sql
```

Execute the generated script with sqlcmd:

```
# sqlcmd -S ServerName -U sa -i ./ScriptName.sql
```

The export/import procedure is something that database professionals deal with on a daily basis, and you should spend some time to master those skills. Also, it is certain that at some point in time, the GUI tool will show up to help you with those tasks, but remember we are talking about the Linux world, where command-line tools are highly appreciated.

DBFS tool

Like in the previous case, this tool is open source, where its purpose is to fill in the gap in the market and prepare the field of SQL Server on Linux for the official arrival.

I believe you have noticed, while reading previous chapters, that SQL Server had a large number of **DMVs (dynamic management views)** that help DBAs and admins to monitor SQL Server internals (live or stored system metadata). SQL Server on Windows, through SSMS, can easily access DMVs and use them. Yes, you can use them with `sqlcmd`, but the problem is that it is hard to list them all in human-readable form. This is the place where DBFS (`https://github.com/Microsoft/dbfs`) jumps in.

In a nutshell, DBFS uses FUSE to mount SQL Server DMVs in the form of a virtual file system, where you can use the classic bash command and explore SQL Server internals. In case you don't know, FUSE allows nonprivileged Linux users to create their own file system without messing with kernel code.

Here are the quick steps for the installation on Kubuntu, as well as a usage scenario:

```
# sudo wget
https://github.com/Microsoft/dbfs/releases/download/0.1.5/dbfs_0.1.5_amd64.
deb
# sudo dpkg -i dbfs_0.1.5_amd64.deb
# sudo apt-get install -f
```

1. Change the directory to where you want to create your config file. In my case, this is home:

   ```
   # cd
   ```

2. Create a directory for the DMVs to mount to:

   ```
   # mkdir dmv
   ```

3. Create the configuration file:

   ```
   # touch dmvtool.config
   ```

4. Edit the `.config` file using your favorite editor.
5. The contents of the file should be:

   ```
   [server name]
   hostname=[HOSTNAME]
   username=[DATBASE_LOGIN]
   password=[PASSWORD]
   version=[VERSION]
   ```

6. Run the tool (this is based on my settings):

   ```
   # dbfs -c ./dmvtool.config -m ./dmv
   ```

7. Enter the dmv folder:

   ```
   # cd dmv
   ```

8. Type `ls`, and you should see your `[server name]`. Now, enter the `[server name]` folder:

   ```
   # cd [server name]
   ```

9. Type `ls`, and you should see a large number of files. I will use MC to illustrate this:

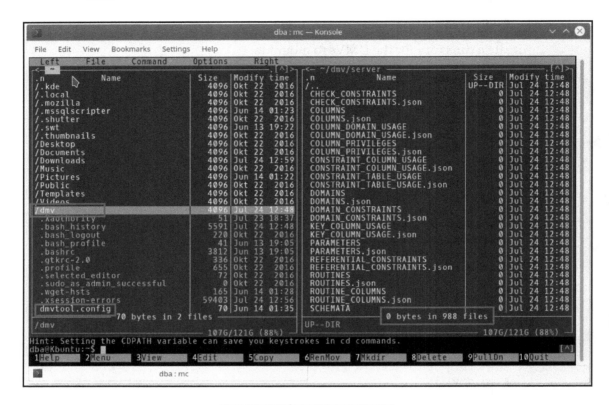

Figure 12-2. DBFS after installation and configuration

Now take a look at the following figure, where we will first list all DMVs with `host` in their name and then call a JSON version of `dm_os_host_info.json`.

Each DMV has a classic and JSON version, so you can use it based on your preferences. I found that the JSON version is a little bit more human-readable:

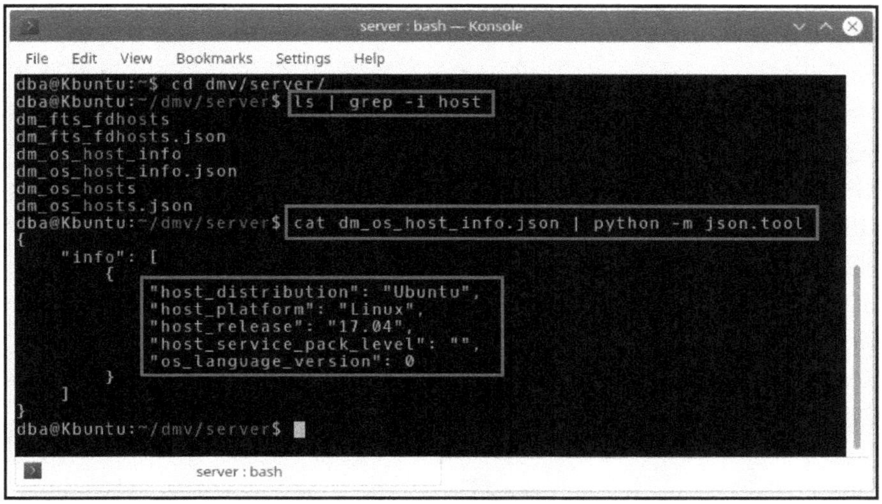

Figure 12-3. DBFS in action

Like any other open source project, DBFS will evolve and adapt based on the user usage, experience, and suggestions for improvements. I advise that you point your web browser to a URL of a product from time to time to check what is going on in the development process, and if you are a developer, you can take an active role in that process.

DBeaver – third party tool

Last but not least, DBeaver (`http://dbeaver.jkiss.org/`) is a very cool multiplatform GUI frontend that can help you with your daily tasks if you are not such a big fan of the command line. Yes, sometimes sqlcmd is necessary and better, but why use it when we have the luxury not to?

So why have we chosen DBeaver? First, it is open source, free, and supports many different SQL and NoSQL databases. SQL Server is just one name on the big list:

- SQL Server
- MySQL
- Oracle
- PostgreSQL

- IBM DB2
- Access
- Sybase
- Java DB
- Firebird
- Derby
- SQLite
- Mimer
- HSQLDB
- H2
- IBM Informix
- Teradata
- SAP MAX DB
- Cache
- Ingres
- Linter
- Vertica
- MongoDB
- Cassandra

If you're a database professional, or you are intending to be, then there is a big chance that you will have at least two or more different databases installed on your workstation. This might lead you to believe that DBeaver is the right tool for you.

 While I am writing this book, SQL Server on Linux is passing from an early development stage to the near final CTP 1.3 - RC1 stage. SQL Server on Linux still does not have an official GUI administration/development tool.

The installation process is quite easy. From the official page, download the version that corresponds to your Linux distribution. The list of packages and supported platforms is shown in the next screenshot:

Figure 12-4. DBeaver download page

You can use Linux Debian packages for Ubuntu/Kubuntu and Linux RPM for SLES/openSUSE.

After you download this, you can use the following command to install it. I am using the RPM 64 package to install it on openSUSE:

```
# sudo rpm -ivh dbeaver-<version-number>.rpm
```

After it is done, just type the following command:

```
# dbeaver &
```

The next step is to configure the connection to your database server. In our case, it is Microsoft SQL Server:

Figure 12-5 Choosing the database server

Now you will need to enter the configuration details: host name, port, username, passwords, and so on. In this phase, DBeaver can download additional database providers based on your choices. This step is illustrated on the next figure:

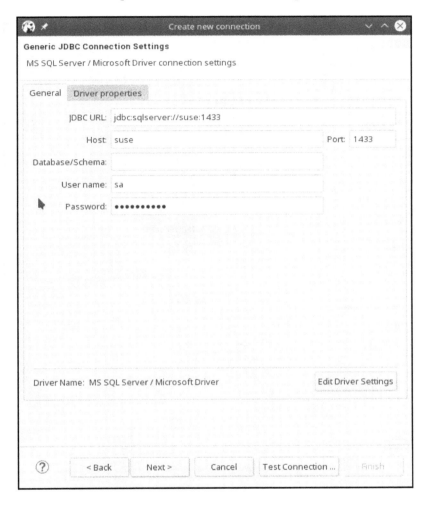

Figure 12-6 Connection parameters

At any moment, you can click on **Test Connection** to check if DBeaver is communicating with your SQL Server before you finish the configuration steps.

In the near-final step, you can name your connection, save the password with the configuration, and choose some additional settings that can help you later. This step is illustrated in the next figure:

Figure 12-7 Additional parameters

After you click **Finish**, you will get a really cool working environment where you can learn, test, and improve your SQL Server on Linux skills:

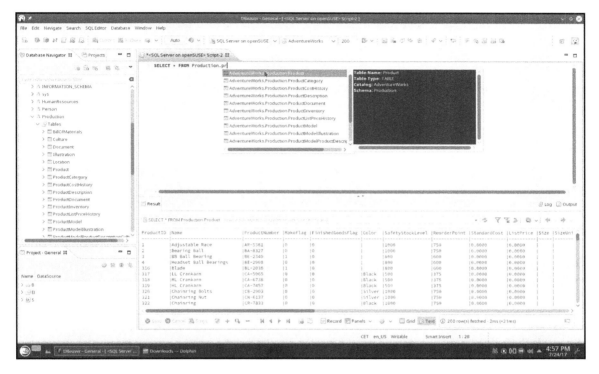

Figure 12-8 DBeaver environment

Every example from this book can be tested through sqlcmd and DBeaver. I suggest that you use both of them. You will need to improve your command-line skills, and sqlcmd is a Spartan environment just for that: clean, efficient, and fast.

While we are waiting for the official Microsoft GUI tool, DBeaver is more than enough to give you Windows luxury on a Linux platform using SQL Server on Linux. As I said before, DBeaver is not the only tool for this, but it is free, open source, and frequently updated.

Summary

In this chapter, you have learned something that goes beyond the traditional relational database concept. SQL Server features, such as query store and temporal databases, will give you more than enough ideas for what SQL Server is capable of.

We also had a quick journey through some additional toolsets that will expand SQL Server's capabilities for you.

Conclusion

We have reached the end of this book, but this is not the end of your journey and your exploration of this new and uncharted area. You are a witness to the creation of a new ecosystem inside the world of Linux that is heavily based on SQL Server on Linux.

This technology is just beginning, and this book is only a quick reference to provide you with a fresh and efficient start. New features will pop up quickly after the final release of SQL Server 2017 and its subversion, SQL Server on Linux. So far, we only have a database engine and integration services. It means that a lot more will come in the future, and this fact is a good thing for this book.

A second version is planned shortly after the final release to fill up the gaps that are missing and things that were not finished in the penultimate phase of development (CTP 1.3 - RC1).

On the other end, I hope that you have enjoyed reading this book as much as I have enjoyed writing this content. The most important thing is that you have benefited from reading this book, and have gained knowledge and skills that you can apply in your future work.

Index

www.ingramcontent.com/pod-product-compliance
Lightning Source LLC
Chambersburg PA
CBHW060554060326
40690CB00017B/3704